THE

WOW
FACTOR

Other Books by William O'Malley

Building Your Own Conscience, RCL-Benzinger

Choosing to Be Catholic, Ave Maria Press

Daily Prayers for Busy People, Liguori Publications

Dare to Dream, Ave Maria Press

The Fifth Week, Loyola Press

God: The Oldest Question, Loyola Press

Help My Unbelief, Orbis Books

Holiness, Orbis Books

Lenten Prayers for Busy People, Orbis Books

Matthew, Mark, Luke, and You, Ave Maria Press

Meeting the Living God, Paulist Press

More Daily Prayers for Busy People, Liguori Publications

On Your Mark, Liturgical Press

Redemptive Suffering, Crossroad Publishing Company

Sacraments: Rites of Passage, RCL-Benzinger

Soul of a Christian Man, Ave Maria Press

The Voice of Blood, Orbis Books

Why Be Catholic, Crossroad Publishing Company

Why Not? Alba House

THE **WOW** FACTOR

Bringing the Catholic Faith to Life

WILLIAM J. O'MALLEY

*"Truly I tell you,
unless you change
and become like children,
you will never enter
the kingdom of heaven."*

ORBIS BOOKS

Maryknoll, New York 10545

Copyright © 2011 by William J. O'Malley.

Published by Orbis Books, Maryknoll, New York 10545-0302.

Queries regarding rights and permissions should be addressed to
Orbis Books, P.O. Box 302, Maryknoll, NY 10545-0302.

Manufactured in the United States of America.

Library of Congress Cataloging-in-Publication Data

O'Malley, William J.
    The wow factor : bringing the Catholic faith to life / William J. O'Malley.
      p. cm.
    ISBN 978-1-57075-927-7 (pbk.)
    1. Catholic Church – Doctrines. 2. Theology, Doctrinal – Popular works.
    3. Catholic Church – Customs and practices. I. Title.
    BX1754.O44 2011
    230'.2 – dc22   2010038236

For
Fr. Michael Nagle

On a clear day
How it will astound you,
That the glow of your being
Outshines every star.

—Alan Jay Lerner

Contents

Why Read This Book?

I was brought up as a Catholic and went to church every week and took the sacraments. It never really touched the core of my being. — STING

My religious education was like packing a bag when the house is on fire. The prospect of the exams — and their definitive effect on my self-esteem — eradicated all perspective. I wasn't ticked off enough at religion back then to give it a good shaking. I just "took it."

Without felt curiosity — doubt, rebellion, skepticism, genuine puzzlement, disillusionment — genuine learning will never happen. Never.

Besides, pondering God is an adult activity. Unfortunately, just when our minds got to a stage where we could actually *do* that, formal consideration of the God questions just...stopped. We now had to knuckle down to *really* important questions, like spouses, children, food. Finding out how to make a living tyrannized over finding out what the hell living is *for.*

We're educated. And Catholic. But probably very few are educated Catholics.

- Subjects we were forced to undergo were just so much potential garbage. They taught us patient politeness (just like Mass), little more. They didn't help with the rent. Or sex.

- Back then, religion was just a resented crimp on our freedom. The questions authentic religion deals with (gratitude, purpose, forgiveness, death) hadn't become gut-troublesome. We hadn't been hurt enough to feel personally threatened by them.

• Even if you finished formal education only five years ago, human understanding of ourselves and our surroundings has doubled since then. At least a hundred times.

Very likely, there was never any "Wow!" in religion back then. Was there ever? What was it in Catholicism that made so many resolute nobodies become somebodies?

This book is about all the things that should have happened at confirmation and almost certainly *didn't:* all the furious winds and tongues of fire that Pentecost meant to the first Christians confirmed. Not our fault they didn't happen. We were simply psychologically incapable of appreciating or comprehending or assimilating or manifesting them. Nor was the official Church. Freedom, enthusiasm, joy weren't programmable. In fact, they were, well, "odd."

The book is also for folks who felt they'd closed the iron door on *any* "thunder thoughts" years ago. But if in the recent past you've found yourself wondering sort of vaguely, "Where in God's name is all this going," this book might help finding a map for the Quest, a felt reason to keep moving forward. And saying, "Wow!" about doing it.

Willingness to surrender to wonder is resurrecting.

The Death of "Wow!"

Is that all there is?
Is that all there is?
If that's all there is, my friends,
Let's keep on dancing.
Let's break out the booze and have
a ball,
if that's all
there is.   — PEGGY LEE

A wise old Jewish comic once said, "Father, we've lost the taste of bread." Too true. Nowadays, bread's nothing without something tangy on it. Wine's just "there," unless you have too much. Until recently when they became (possibly) threatened, no one really cared much about such miracles as air and water. We still drive one-to-a-car and chuck cans out the window.

What's probably more dismaying to those who think beyond their own skins is that even undeniably spectacular events no longer can excite. Long before they were canceled (perhaps from lack of public interest), moon landings had become passé. After a while, media overkill made the BP oil leakage in the Gulf of Mexico seem more tedious than shocking. Unless a concert has apocalyptic strobes and explosions and smoke, they're so-so.

Since humans first evolved into reflective beings, we've been assaulted by miracles from every side: the sun and stars, the thrash of the rain, the stunning intrusions of birth and death, the bewildering/intoxicating mystery of sex, the infinitely changing treasury of faces we brush past every day. But our brains are vised between the iPods or spuriously connected to someone trust-worthy through the cellphone. (I once saw a boy and girl crossing the campus hand-in-hand, each on a portable phone. I prayed it wasn't to one another.) Immanuel Kant is credited with saying, "If the stars came out only once in a lifetime, we'd stay up all that night." Now we stay up late in Plato's cave just to watch the enervated stars on *The Tonight Show.*

In the silent, isolated depths, each separate self gradually thick-ens the tough crustacean shell of his or her own individual self-protectiveness. We shock-absorb our selves with soporifics — television, music, dope, booze — to anesthetize our fears and what we judge is our woeful inadequacy in the face of unending chal-lenge. We can lose ourselves in shallow Darwinian contests like *Survivor, American Idol,* and *The Bachelor*, as if they were as pro-found as the *Odyssey.* We can lose ourselves along with 50 million others, watching eleven men carry an inflated pig bladder through eleven other men, down a big lawn with white stripes. A game for children becomes desperately important, and those who play it skillfully get paid forty times more than the president of the United States, who can send us into oblivion with the push of a button. Even the arts, like dance and drama, can be turned into a lucrative contest that depends as much on looks, charm, and pandering to the common tastes as a national election. These are struggles as elemental as gladiatorial combats in the arena. But combats without death. There is, in fact, no death anymore. That happens only in the secrecy of hospitals and nursing homes. And the genuine deaths on the news are no more real than the staged deaths on *NCIS.* Therefore, the Gospel promise of resurrection, of freedom from the fear of death, becomes utterly meaningless.

We protect ourselves with busy-ness — grooming, sports, secu-rity blanket electronics. It's as if, without being able to verbalize it, we awakened in the world of Samuel Beckett's desolate clowns and, like them, have to fill the airless emptiness with chatter and games, self-deceptive distractions. We forget that for centuries, being "distracted" was a synonym for "insane."

All the comfortable old signposts are down: the presidency, the Church, the schools. The only heroes are the amoral ones: rock stars and athletes, whose contemptuous self-indulgences can be overlooked, since they are up there on the stage and the tube — where it's really at. One must fill the void in order to forget that Mr. Godot will not come this evening. Or tomorrow evening. "Then keep on dancing. Let's break out the booze . . . and have . . . a ball. If that's all . . . there is."

Given the choice, would we honestly hope our young become like Donald Trump or Julia Roberts rather than like Martin Luther King or Mother Teresa — with all those firehoses and police dogs, all those irksome leeches and lepers? And where did they get that revulsion for heroism? Year after year now, when I give a questionnaire that includes the question: "Who are your heroes?" three-quarters consistently leave that blank or write, "I have no heroes." How could they, in a *National Enquirer* ethos? And we have allowed them to become like that: the future.

What are the things anybody can say "Wow!" about today? Mountains? Stars? Babies? Books? Beer? The sheer gift of just being alive? Not very many, since awareness of our fragile grasp on those realities is isolated from both the urban and suburban. The media have made the trivial important (image, numbers, notoriety), and the important trivial (sex, love, death). We shun anything genuinely frightening or unnerving. Despite the evident popularity of so-called "reality" TV shows, T. S. Eliot still rings true: "Humankind cannot bear too much reality." Fifty years ago, the idealistic young were actually rioting and risking their personal safety to protest the Vietnam War. Today, few are willing to protest two wars in Afghanistan and Iraq in which more lives have been lost than in the suicide attacks they were meant to avenge. In an age of such indifference, what in God's name can be called exciting? Or meaningful? Or even significant?

Our ethos at least seems to be settling for mere stimulation — and simulation. Like being tickled, agitating a nerve, instead of being genuinely happy. And it's everywhere we turn: "Full of sound and fury, signifying nothing."

In general, I believe the death of "Wow!" is based on that same fear that is at the root of all those defenses I spoke of before. We feel awe only when we are caught off guard — by the greatness of something other than ourselves. And we're rarely going to be caught off our guard. It's called "paranoia." Awe happens only when the greatness of the other makes us feel automatically and rightfully small. Before a great hulk of mountain, before the unceasing power of the ocean, before the enormity of the heavens ablaze with stars, we are brought to our knees. And we feel very small and vulnerable on our knees.

When you consider the vastness of space, even an empire on earth is inconsequential. Then what of me? When you consider the age of the universe, even a life of a hundred years is trivial. Then what of me? When you consider the Library of Congress, numberless volumes that house the accumulated wrestling of humankind for truth, even the minds of Aristotle and Aquinas and Einstein pale. Then what of me? It might redeem one's value to realize that, in all that vastness, no matter how infinitesimal I *seem*, an Infinite God has sought me out, called my name, dotes on me. And yet that, too, could make me feel small, dependent, indebted. And there is the un-coolest state of all: to be thought holy. Better to be called "loser" than to be thought "holy."

It's better to withdraw with a few friends into the nutshell, insulated by the mirrors, and not think of such things, connected to the really real world electronically. True, the mind and spirit by their nature are hungry, but they can be palliated by junk food: TV and tabloids for the mind, rock concerts and unsportive sports for the spirit. Even sex can be mere anesthesia.

We were born curious, our eyes and minds and fingers seemingly insatiable. We were born for frontiers: the unexplored grass at the edge of the baby blanket. The inborn spirit of human-kind must search, must outgrow pampering. But gradually, almost by some perverse conspiracy of protectiveness, we become dis-spirited: "Don't touch!" "Keep off the grass!" "Beware of strangers!" "Is there a money-back guarantee?" The schools turn wonder into drudgery and uniqueness into aberration. Acceptance by the dulled others becomes worth almost any surrender, and nothing is worth the price of solitude: to read, to ponder, to paint, to pray. In the new Plato's cave, we have the electronic shadows to make the unreal true and to give us an ersatz peace — even though every ad ever produced is deliberately formulated to make us unhappy.

After the liberation from inquisitiveness, the irredeemably curi-ous stick out as indeed curious — weird, outlandish, changelings. In "normal" people, imagination, what makes us truly human, has been banked down and finally smothered, and we are left as what the new atheists like Christopher Hitchens and Richard Dawkins diminish us to being: apes implanted with computers, canny heads and candid loins, shuttling from *Fortune* to *Playboy*. As C. S. Lewis called us, we become "men without chests," plump in the prison of mediocrity. And so, sick with self-protectiveness, the heart and the spirit die.

There's nothing like the exhilaration of having climbed the mountain, step by bloody step, and crawling up the final few feet — and there it is! Wow! But what joy is there when we can afford to take a helicopter to the top or watch passively while someone else does it for us on the TV? Since the dawn of intelligence, men and women have achieved the fullness of their humanity only by freely committing themselves to challenge. Dig-nity and worth are purchased only at the price of pain, which is why we sit enviously hypnotized by the Olympics: "the joy of vic-tory and the agony of defeat." Comfortingly, it is someone else's agony; dis-spiritingly, it is also someone else's joy. What's more, it seems trivial to compare the conquest of a ski run with the conquest of the true challenges of being human: the challenges of one's own mind and one's own heart. But those can readily be short-circuited by the distractions.

Those two challenges — our own mind and our own heart — without comforting rules and protective officials and time limits, are a horrifying prospect to the self-doubting, the comfortable, the spoiled — in a word: us. Think of how frightening it is, then, to hear: "Unless you lose your life, you will never find it." Think of how unintelligible it is to call a book *The Good News*, when it claims that resurrection comes only after Calvary. In a world where even inconvenience is insupportable, where instant gratification takes too long, imagine what would happen in your family if the electricity were cut off for a month.

As an educator — and especially as a religious educator — I believe my job of evangelizing the cautiously comfortable is far more difficult than that of my sisters and brothers who try to evangelize the destitute heathen. The gospel of materialism is paganism, but without the awe. True pagans are so awed by the powers of the earth that they're bowing all the time — to the god in the waterfall, to the god in the thunder, to the god who provides the grain and the game. But — in all honesty — to what do we allow ourselves to bow?

Consider *liberating vulnerability*. Resurrection from security. Resurrection to passion.

I am trying to sell a very unpopular attitude: surrender. Not passivity, but exposure, yielding, susceptibility: to the truths about our giftedness, to the needs of others, to God. If knowing and loving make one truly human (more than merely highly specialized animals or savages), then vulnerability is the precondition of fulfilled humanity. *To know* means that I am vulnerable to the truth, humble before it, no matter where the truth leads or how unpleasant (or demanding) it is to accept. *To love* means that I am vulnerable to the other, humble before them, no matter how inconvenient their calls for help, no matter how they hurt me.

Even if I must hurt them, for their own sake, I subordinate their loving me — or even liking me — in order to love them. But which of our young will risk being disliked? (Perhaps part of the reason for that is that we ourselves have shuddered from being disliked rather than love them in ways they need.)

Selling vulnerability to the cautiously comfortable is like selling cancer. Yet to be exalted, we must be humbled (Matt. 23:12). "Thrall" means "slave," therefore to "be enthralled" requires vulnerability. John Donne captured that ultimate paradox, "Batter my heart, three-personed God . . . for I, except you enthrall me, never shall be free, nor ever chaste except you ravish me."

What I am asking is that we paw away all the unquestioned defenses that have buried us in self-protectiveness — which not only warded off the anguish that plagued the poor since the rigor of the caves but also rejected what made their lives more meaning-filled than ours.

Schooling now abjures any hint of regard for what makes us different from other animals — the soul — because even the word summons accusations of imposing religion. Such powerful resistance to spirituality is, clearly, stupid. Whether there is a Supreme Being or not, even the fiercest atheists want their children to be decent, moral, humane. Science may be able to prove chemicals and electricity spontaneously generated human self-awareness, but I defy it to explain evident realities materialist scientism would scorn, all those specifically human activities simpler folk associated with the soul: honor, selfless love, wisdom, virtue, humor, the need for a reason, meaning, purpose. None of those activities is reducible merely to the body or the brain — both of which we share with other animals. Monogamous marriage is not rational, neither is having children — though neither of them is *ir*-rational; they are *beyond* rational. To say strict logic is the only way to truth is reductionism in the highest degree. Truth > facts.

Biologist Richard Dawkins writes, almost huffily:

We humans have purpose on the brain. We find it hard to look at anything without wondering what it is "for," what the motive for it is, or the purpose behind it. When the obsession with purpose becomes pathological it is called paranoia — reading malevolent purpose into what is actually random bad luck. But this is just an exaggerated form of a nearly universal delusion.

The core of humanity, dismissed as merely bothersome, like an appendix.

We are the only creatures we know who are aware we are selves, able to use the future tense, to regret. Other animals know facts, that danger is near, but don't seem to ask *why.* They give their lives for their own but not, like us, for a principle or for people we don't even like. Only we have hungers not rooted in a needful body or coldly rational mind: to be honorable, to find meaning, to survive death. Ignoring those indisputable facts is the rankest reductionism.

My patron saint as a teacher is Annie Sullivan, who for what seemed like forever drew the liberating signs in Helen Keller's uncomprehending hands, trying to tell her she wasn't the only person, that an immeasurably more exciting world was outside her cocoon of safe, self-enclosed darkness. And Annie trusted that somehow, somewhere, there would be the moment of vision.

And it came, in that incandescent moment at the pump when Helen made the most liberating of all human discoveries. Poor, frightened girl. She discovered that she was not alone.

That's what "grace" means.

Freedom from Sacred and Sinful

Things fall apart; the centre cannot hold;
Mere anarchy is loosed upon the world,
The blood-dimmed tide is loosed, and everywhere
The ceremony of innocence is drowned;
The best lack all conviction, while the worst
Are full of passionate intensity....
And what rough beast, its hour come round at last
Slouches towards Bethlehem to be born?

— WILLIAM BUTLER YEATS

When a woman sits weeping in the ER with a young intern who just told her that her twelve-year-old son has died of a brain hemorrhage, she mumbles, "But why?" The young intern has given her "the answer," hasn't he? Her son's fall caused swelling in the brain — cerebral edema. The pooled blood increased pressure on nearby brain tissue, and the reduced blood-flow shut down his brain. But she keeps weeping and wondering, "Why?" For all his learning, the intern simply doesn't even comprehend what she's asking.

Check out the entry for "love" in the dictionary: about forty fine-print lines defining the one reality that supposedly makes facing the poopstorm worth the effort, and ask yourself if it really rises to that challenge. Does it even hint at what real love *costs?*

This is a book for people who have spent a lot of time looking for *causes* — what's gotten into my spouse, am I too easy on the kids, what can get me a raise, what's that thumping in the attic?

9

This is a time to probe down to a deeper level: What's *really* making me moody? Why are people so unreadable at times? What reasons can I give the kids for reading Shakespeare when I never read it myself? Am I "livin' good" without "living well"? Where did all the "zing" go? Why do the really important things cost so much more than money? Time to search out *reasons*.

Over the centuries, Something Very Powerful has built a bulwark between the meaning of "intellect" and "intelligence." (Some put the blame, too glibly, solely on Alpha males.) At its simplest, *intellect* connotes knowing a lot of stuff, taking things apart, rationality, diagnosing and defining—the "masculine" left brain. *Intelligence* sees patterns where most people see chaos, putting things together, intuition, understanding and depth—the "feminine" right brain. If you have a tax problem, you want an intellect; if you have a moral (human) problem, you want an intelligence. If you need a diagnosis of a pain in your gut, or if someone you love just died, or if you're contemplating a preemptive war, it's reassuring to find *both* in the same person, not someone who's working half-wittedly. Intellect can give you causes; intelligence—wisdom—can try to give you reasons.

SATs and IQ tests are, really, intellect tests, evidencing your grasp of facts and your skills in manipulating them. They decide who appears on *Jeopardy* and who sits puzzled but applauding. Wisdom can be tested only in going beyond reasoning (which wise folk still consider essential) and finding out if the conclusion works out in practice. It's why we have libraries, so we don't all have to start from scratch. It's why parents — even uneducated ones—can predict that such-and-such behavior will almost certainly end up badly. Not necessarily brainy; "just" wise.

But that Something Very Powerful dislikes ambiguity, gray areas, compromise, paradox, so it sets up an antagonism inside the same skulls between the inborn humans-only potentials for *both* rationality *and* intuition.

Once prosperity had given the Greeks the leisure to ponder both causes and reasons, their Olympian gods seemed like no more than an embarrassing dysfunctional family. So their wisest thinkers purged the earthiness of their pagan gods and replaced them with abstract ideas. Then the Romans were even more hardnosed and practical; they knew the effectiveness of gold and fear, and to all intents substituted "The State" for the gods. Later, despite their evident Christian faith, Copernicus and Galileo at least seemed to threaten the reliability of scripture as a privileged insight into God and God's notions of what humans were made for and how they could legitimately act. In seeking to overthrow the unarguable flaws and excesses of the visible Church, the Reformation gradually broke down the walls of dogmas binding under threat of death and damnation and — effectively — shattered the cohesion not only of a worldwide institution but also of a pretty much universal and seamless system of beliefs, sacred and secular. In the eighteenth century, the Enlightenment, revolutions, and the broadening scope of literacy and printed books widened the gap between the two contentious ways of understanding, rightly allowing anyone (at least most males) an opinion — but concomitantly giving rise to the quite questionable belief that "my opinion's as good as anyone else's!" No matter how unsubstantiated or ill-considered it is. Many mistakenly believed (and still believe) that is what democracy guarantees. In the Industrial Revolution that followed, machines began to emerge to begin the deification of a new god: efficiency. As Dickens's Mr. Gradgrind asserted about children in his company school: "Teach these boys and girls nothing but Facts. Facts alone are wanted in life. Plant nothing else, root out everything else. You can form the minds of reasoning animals only upon Facts: nothing else will ever be of service to them."

Many of Dickens's readers didn't realize he was mocking poor benighted Gradgrind. They thought he made eminent good sense.

Today's education systems agree. So do most parents (and, reluctantly, students): "You need an education [read: diploma] to get a good job."

Human beings began to be treated within the reductionist limits so many worthy philosophers had confined them to: rational animals, computer-driven apes, freed from airy, "womanish" suppositions like the heart and soul. At the same time, Utilitarianism introduced the resultant and quite appealing belief that the morality of any action depended not on any objective reality within the victim and perpetrator, but solely on the outcome. Since even before the Greeks, the touchstone of morality had been, "Is this right?" Now the sole norm for human choices was: "Does it work?" — which, in turn, led to justifying, "Can we get away with this?"

Therefore, unadulterated science (scientism) freed nature from any *inherent* purposes, stripped reality down to manageable parts, "factors." In society, human beings were competitors and consumers; in war, they were personnel and "casualties," not sons and daughters, husbands and wives. It chose to ignore in humans what had been considered the "natural" values of self-esteem and interpersonal relationships and redefined us in terms of quantifiable values: colorless statistics. Herbert Marcuse wrote: "The historical achievement of science and technology has rendered possible the translation of values into technical tasks — the materialization of values."

After an eviscerating world Depression, World War II generated enormous changes in life for developed nations. Women flooded the work force and found financial and psychological clout; men returning from places they'd never known existed were subsidized through college and moved into a swelling middle-class. Henry Ford shrewdly realized that mass production required mass consumption and therefore wages high enough to motivate spending. Relatively inexpensive vehicles and expanding road systems created a new suburban culture, which eroded the ghetto mentality and ethnic cultures.

But a previously self-defining group can't be assimilated without being in great part diluted. The goal changed from maintaining a matrix of small-group identity to becoming "like everybody else." All of which gave rise to a whole new ethos: consumerism, a system whose function was to create an insistent desire for more goods and services, minimizing discomforts — even inconvenience. What the American founding fathers referred to as "the pursuit of happiness" transformed into offers to effectively guarantee happiness. For a price.

In 1955, economist Victor Lebow stated:

> Our enormously productive economy demands that we make consumption our way of life, that we convert the buying and use of goods into rituals, that we seek our spiritual satisfaction and our ego satisfaction in consumption. We need things consumed, burned up, worn out, replaced and discarded at an ever-increasing rate.

And then came television. In Paddy Chayevsky's *Network* (1976), one character tells another, a cold-heartedly successful TV executive: "You are television incarnate, Diana, indifferent to suffering, insensitive to joy. All of life is reduced to the common rubble of banality." Before they reach kindergarten, children will now have absorbed more gore and mayhem from TV and video games than a veteran in the army of Genghis Khan, to the point that suffering and death have no sting. (Forget resurrection.) Every ten minutes, no matter what the product, long before they can think, a voice cajoles them, "The more things you have, the happier you'll be." Keeping alive their infantile greed well into adulthood and beyond — even to the cost of their funerals. Scripted programs establish that no one has sex unless they're *un*-married. Every mystery should wrap up in an hour. They embody a life no human ever has lived or can, so that the unattainable becomes necessary. "Reality" shows demonstrate that, if you want to win, you've got to screw your friends.

In Stalin's Russia, such psychological manipulation was called "brainwashing" and was despised by anyone with a shred of humanity. Today however, in developed countries, such psychic enslavement is simply good business. No wonder the suicide rate of affluent teenagers is so high. They've been promised that the world can give them what the world simply can't give.

But Chayevsky meant a much larger, more powerful and insidious "network" than the TV enterprises we understand. A representative of the conglomerate that owns the TV system says:

> You have meddled with the primal forces of nature, Mr. Beall! And I won't have it! Is that clear? . . . There are no nations; there is only one, holistic system of systems, vast and immense, inter-woven, interacting, a multinational domin- ion of dollars! It is the international system of currency which determines the quality of life on this planet. . . . There is no democracy. There is no America. There is IBM and ITT and ATT and Dupont, Dow, and Exxon. Those are the nations today. . . . The world is a business, Mr. Beall!

Again, try to imagine what would happen to your family and neighborhood if the electricity went out for a month. A year?

In trying to comprehend the evil of the Nazi camps and the ordinary people who designed them, supplied them, and main- tained them, Hannah Arendt wrote in *Eichmann in Jerusalem* that the root of inhumanity was not some extratemporal devil or a foolish pair of nudists in a Garden or some "bad seed." The perpetrators were not fanatics or sociopaths. They left work and played Mozart and would never kick their neighbor's nasty dog. Just ordinary folks, following orders. The root of human degrada- tion is the sheer banality of most human minds — the dullness, insipidity, the common unquestioned acceptance of the rat race. As George tries to tell Lenny in *Of Mice and Men*, it's not wicked people that cause all the trouble; it's dumb people. And "dumb" has nothing to do with IQ. Oedipus was the epitome of intellect, but "dumb." He had keen eyes, but not true "vision." He never entertained even the remotest possibility he might be wrong. He was a complete narcissist. He lacked *perspective.* They called him wise, but he was only smart.

Today we find ourselves besieged by a world that thrives on catering to narcissism — enlightened self-interest, continual self-absorption, the dominance of image over substance — in the marketplace, education, entertainment, sports. News reporting — which had for so long prided itself on independence from image and earnings — fell subservient to popularity and profit. Even parenting became a ladder to define personal success — and not just for the children: scrambling to get preschool places when the child is still in Pampers or even *in utero,* tutoring and testing for excuses and remedies for merely moderate performance, SAT prep classes, fathers asking how to "market my kids" to colleges.

Philosophical values seem to contribute nothing to the subjugation of nature and its profitability, and in fact they too often hinder progress. When you face the practical problems of constructing an atomic bomb, for instance, including human victims into the equation can be distracting.

Somewhere along the line, to get rid of ambiguity and cloudy thinking, to simplify life so even the mentally challenged could grasp its purpose, reason took precedence over all other ways of knowing, education became efficient schooling for jobs, philosophy became rigidly pragmatic, god became the Economy, in whose name any choice is justified. World War I soldiers had a saying, "Leave the thinking to the officers and the horses. They have bigger heads." Somewhere, the humanizing heart and soul got ground under the wheels of progress.

Liberation from the Gods

When we got rid of the gods — effectively if not admittedly — we sacrificed a sense of the sacredness of life in order to rid ourselves of the paralyzing tyranny of guilt. Without the gods, "anything is permitted." But when you get rid of guilt, what you get is Auschwitz.

The sheerly utilitarian life-view peeled away all "womanish" sentimentality. One down-to-earth Nazi propagandist concluded that the average human body contains sufficient fat to make seven cakes of soap, enough iron to make a medium-sized nail, phosphorus adequate to make two thousand match-heads, enough sulphur to rid oneself of fleas. The camps rented out prisoners as slaves to such still thriving enterprises as BMW, Siemens, and Thyssen-Krupp for six Reichsmarks a day, minus a half-mark for food, multiplied by "average life of prisoner" (270 days), plus "rational disposal of corpse (fillings, clothes, bones)." The tally comes to RM 1,690 — about $670 today. Paltry. But not when multiplied by 15 million.

To try to understand such routine inhumanity, in the early 1960s Stanley Milgram, a Yale professor of psychology, carried out experiments on the effect of punishment on learning. A subject was strapped to an "electric chair," and each time the subject missed a memory question, a paid volunteer pressed a button to deliver a shock, intensifying at each wrong answer until the final calibration: "Danger: Brain Damage." Cries of the subject increased from murmurs, to pleas, to shrieks of pain. Actually, the experiment was not about learning but obedience. The "subject" was an actor who suffered no pain. The real subjects were the volunteers at the console: how far would they go before compassion refused obedience? Before the experiment, Milgram circularized specialists asking how many of a thousand teachers would go all the way to "Danger: Brain Damage." Their estimate was one-tenth of 1 percent. Actually, 62 percent obeyed the commands when Milgram took full responsibility, in writing. Teachers!

On March 16, 1968, U.S. soldiers led by Lt. William L. Calley invaded the Vietnamese hamlet of My Lai, an alleged Vietcong stronghold. But the peasants had been warned, so when the unit arrived no one was left but those who couldn't run: old people and infants. Nonetheless, since orders were to "shoot anything that moves," American soldiers dutifully shot to death 347 unarmed civilians, then the cattle. Evidently, no one involved spoke of it, since the incident did not become public until a full year later. Five soldiers were court martialed, and Calley was sentenced to life at hard labor. But in September 1974, a federal court overturned the conviction and set Calley free, since he was only following orders. Whoever devised the mission, and gave the orders, and supplied the means was lost somewhere in the anonymity of military bureaucracy.

The event was horrific, and the question was how young men of a supposedly civilized society could so lose their humanity, their souls. However, had they killed far more people over a larger area, impersonally from overhead, with bombs, smart rockets, white phosphorous, and napalm, they would have been following what is common military practice today, and the society that issued their weapons and their orders could remain complacent of its rightness.

Lost Souls

In the old days, speaking of "losing your soul" meant at the end of life plunging into an eternal inferno populated by sadistic fiends working ungodly torments on adulterers, murderers, perjurers, and archbishops Dante didn't care for. Even after the easements of Vatican II, it seems such images are still rooted deeply in the world's imagination. Sometimes, though, it becomes so outlandish or even just plain silly that people who have found education and sophistication say, "T'hell with it." Just as the Golden Age Greeks bade snickering farewell to the Zeus family. Atheists and agnostics have a truth that even believers ought to deal with: Morality has nothing whatever to do with religion. Religion is a relationship with a deity, if such an entity exists. But—

beyond dispute — anyone can do moral evil, even if there is no God. Morality is a web of relationships we have with every other inhabitant of this planet and the planet itself. Morality means "being a decent human," more accountable than any rock or rose or rattlesnake. The Golden Rule — treating others as oneself — is embedded almost verbatim in almost every philosophy ever formulated. It is not a matter of religion but of human survival.

What changed over these centuries is not what being human *is* but what those who spend their lives thinking thunder thoughts *believe* being human means — and advise us to accept. Ideas trickle down from the ivory towers, to the graduate schools, to colleges, and thence into *Time* and *Parade* and Rush Limbaugh. And most accept that service gratefully, since thunder thinking takes too long to master and is tedious and time-consuming even if one succeeds at it. In our time, morality became what Dr. Alfred Kinsey called merely "social formalities" or "social restrictions." In such a view, we don't have sex on the front lawn as dogs do merely from fear of what the neighbors might think. Therefore, all customs, laws, and rules are relative, alien, arbitrary, and external to the individual. Sex is a purely biological action that renders all guilt feelings dispensable. You can give exactly the same leeway to plagiarism, sex in the Oval Office, cyber porn, or herding inferior persons into showers to be gassed. And, according to Dr. Kinsey, the more frequently you flaunt the customs, the less the guilt.

In a liberated society, where all opinions must be considered valid, there is inevitably a kind of aloof indifference to the *content* of anyone's belief. All beliefs must be given equal tolerance. Personal opinions are, to this openminded view, self-justifying. That stance, which is quite common, seems not to consider that the most open mind is an empty head. In *My Fair Lady*, Henry Higgins says, "The French never care what they do, actually, as long as they pronounce it properly."

But the Greek word for "sin," *hamartia*, gives a less easily eluded perspective on human behavior. It comes from archery and means "missing the mark," in the case of an individual soul: missing the whole point of having been a human being — never having found the difference between merely surviving and being alive (which is what this whole book is about). Making a living is a ludicrous exercise if you've never even discovered what living is *for.*

In the present-day ethos described so far, the message is, inescapably, that "eternal life" — happiness, fulfillment, success — depends critically on achieving a maximum of money-fame-sex-power. But few pause to reflect that so many who really had those four coveted self-validations "missed the real point." Elvis Presley, Marilyn Monroe, Janis Joplin, Jimi Hendrix, John Belushi, Jim Morrison, River Phoenix, Heath Ledger, and a host of others "had it all," in spades, and yet for years anesthetized themselves with drugs (from life and from themselves). Because they'd discovered the meaning of life and achieved it? Because they were so happy? It makes one pause and reflect. You can "lose your soul" and still keep moving.

Finding himself alone in the godless emptiness, Nietzsche asserted that, if there is no God, then we are God; we find fatuous meaning in asserting ourselves: might *makes* right. Karl Marx offered a brief and spurious value to individuals in contributing to a future workers' paradise they will never witness. In the 1920s, Joseph Conrad's Kurtz found himself devoured by *The Heart of Darkness,* and Franz Kafka's Gregor Samsa woke one morning and discovered he was a great fat bug. During and after World War II, Samuel Beckett's wistful clowns met each evening, Waiting for Godot, killing time before time killed them. Jean-Paul Sartre reacted to the void with *Nausea;* Albert Camus' heroes fired the arm at the impotent nothingness and found consolation in sheer bitchery: "I will *not* quit!"

In a more commonplace desolation, Arthur Miller's Willy Loman and his two sons try to validate themselves by achieving the preposterous "American Dream." He's immovably convinced that "the man who makes an appearance in the business world, the man who creates personal interest, is the man who gets ahead. Be liked and you will never want." All it takes is a shoeshine, a smile, and a firm handshake. In the end, plagued by hallucinations, out of a job, Willy borrows money to pay his insurance and then kills himself so his wife can pay off the mortgage on a house no one will live in. Willy's sons, Biff and Happy, bought the American Dream, too. But Biff can't cope with it, dropping out after high school, going from job to job and one petty theft to another. Now he loves work on a ranch, but he can't be happy because there's no money in it. Happy has a well-paying job, but he beds his friends' fiancées a week before their weddings. His excuse is that "everybody around me is so false that I'm constantly lowering my ideals."

I met a man once who came to me utterly unhappy. He despised his job, and his anger was contagious, threatening his marriage and his relationship with his kids. I asked if he'd ever been happy at his job, and he answered immediately, "Of course! At the job I was promoted from. I couldn't wait to get to work on Mondays." I asked how much he made now, and he said, "Ninety grand." And how much at the previous job: "Seventy-five grand." I asked if he could go to his boss and say he was grateful for the promotion, but could he have his old job back. He looked at me, puzzled. Finally, he said, "You're asking me to give up fifteen grand." Is it making you happy? Is it worth your marriage? We talked twice, an hour each time. But he couldn't give up that fifteen grand. "He went away, grieving, for he had many possessions" (Mark 10:22).

A tribe in Africa traps monkeys for food. They hollow out a gourd with a hole just large enough for a monkey to get its paw inside, where there is some bait monkeys can't resist. But when the monkey's fist has grabbed the bait, it can't get it out of the hole, so rather than let go of its treasure, it starves to death. Many learned people believe monkeys are our cousins. The family resemblance is quite amazing, especially when humans forego precisely what makes us different from monkeys, namely, the ability to deny ourselves satisfaction to save our lives.

Entitlement and Helplessness

The Network keeps reminding us how unfulfilled we are, how great our need still is for what will provide us with the happiness we so richly deserve. But there is always *more*, just out of reach. And like Aesop's fox, we keep leaping up. Working, working, working; buying, buying, buying. But as the Stones realized as far back as 1965: "I Can't Get No Satisfaction!" Our jaws snap just short of the grapes, until after a while, even a willing fool is ready to admit defeat. "They're probably sour." It's frustrating. It threatens our illusions.

Ironically, the more the media widen the scope of our global awareness, the smaller and defensively insulated we become.

A few years ago, a fifteen-year-old boy was arrested for murdering an old woman for about $30. He was asked if he felt in any way ashamed or regretful, and he answered, "Why? She's not me." When serial killer Ted Bundy answered the same question, he reportedly asked what was the fuss? "There are so many people." Jean Twenge quotes a member of what she aptly calls "Generation Me": "I couldn't care less how I'm viewed by society. I live my life according to the morals, views, and standards that I create." And I bet she never ploughed through Nietzsche.

Fifteen million died in Hitler's camps, far more from starvation and overwork than from deliberate gassing. Six million were Jews; the rest were gentiles. Stalin's Great Purge (1936–38) killed 20 million, mostly people who had become educated. Mao's Great Leap Forward (1958–61) killed 30 million in three years. In Rwanda (1995), Hutus killed 800,000 Tutsis in a hundred days because they weren't "like us."

We share the earth with 35 million refugees, more than there are Canadians. Twelve million AIDS orphans live somehow in Africa. Fifty million babies are aborted worldwide each year, twice the population of Iraq. Today, the probability of a first marriage ending in separation or divorce within five years is 20 percent, but the probability of a premarital cohabitation breaking up within five years is 49 percent. One-third of American families are single-parented, and fatherless children are twice as likely to drop out of school, commit 72 percent of adolescent murders, and are eleven times more prone to violent behavior. Today, homicide is the second-leading cause of death for young adults, after car accidents, of which 60 percent are alcohol-related.

> Things fall apart; the centre cannot hold;
> Mere anarchy is loosed upon the world.

This is not the first time in history when everybody knew the world was falling apart. But because of the glut of news pushed into our faces every day about the colossal scope and intensity of horrific events — drive-bys, suicide bombings, terrorism, and the rest — we become insensitive to evil. We notice it now only as we notice litter or graffiti or noise — or commercials, when they are especially blatant: Jeffrey Dahmer, Jonestown, Waco, Oklahoma City, 9/11, the Gulf Spill. And if we are insensitive to the depletion of the ozone layer that would protect our grandchildren from cancer, to an infant murdered every few days in New York City, to the flag-draped caskets returning from Iraq and Afghanistan, how indifferent can we become to our own peccadillos?

Nobody can do anything about anything. It's all just too big and out of whack. I'm nobody — which becomes a self-fulfilling prophecy. Psychologist Robert Johnson writes:

Western people are children of inner poverty, though outwardly we have everything. Probably no other people in history has been so lonely, so alienated, so confused over values, so neurotic. We have dominated our environment with sledge-hammer force and electronic precision. We amass riches on an unprecedented scale. But few of us, very few indeed, are at peace with ourselves, secure in our relationships, content with our loves, or at home in the world.

Freed from superstitions, we have lost our souls. We turn not to devil worship but to anesthesia. We no longer think, as more primitive peoples did, of the earth as our Mother; it's merely dirt under which there may be oil or uranium. The stars lost their divinity as astronomy developed, and there is no need for the blood of Adonis in a world of chemical fertilizers. And we know that the Rebel Without a Cause today is not going to hell. He is going nowhere.

> Tomorrow, and tomorrow, and tomorrow,
> Creeps in this petty pace from day to day
> To the last syllable of recorded time,
> And all our yesterdays have lighted fools
> The way to dusty death. Out, out, brief candle!
> Life's but a walking shadow, a poor player
> That struts and frets his hour upon the stage
> And then is heard no more: it is a tale
> Told by an idiot, full of sound and fury,
> Signifying nothing.   —*Macbeth*, Act 5, Sc. 5

Richard Dawkins writes remorselessly: "This is one of the hardest lessons for humans to learn. We cannot admit things might be neither good nor evil. Neither cruel nor kind, but simply callous — indifferent to all suffering, lacking all purpose."

> *The best lack all conviction, while the worst*
> *Are full of passionate intensity....*

We forget that Martin Luther King, Nelson Mandela, Lech Walesa, Mother Teresa, and anyone else who ever made a difference were once nobodies too. Did they have some secret not taught in schools? Or were they simply misled and self-delusively idealistic?

The very anguish that cries for meaning in a meaningless universe reveals a deep-rooted conviction that there *must* be something that "makes sense of it all." As far as we can tell, no sow shudders to think all her babies will one day die; we do. We suffer from a persistent, universal, humans-only need for meaning, purpose, salvation. It defies the manifest intelligence that separates us from other animals to admit that, of all the entities we know, we are the only ones with a hunger for a food that doesn't exist. Tarrou, a character in Camus' *The Plague*, says of God, "He doesn't exist. The bastard." But what if God did? How truly liberating at the very least to have Someone to blame!

T W O

The Vital Attitude: Humility

And now here is my secret, a very simple secret;
it is only with the heart that one can see rightly.
What is essential is invisible to the eye.
— ANTOINE DE SAINT-EXUPÉRY

Kurt Vonnegut Jr. put the question of happiness succinctly: "What the hell are people *for?*" Labrador retrievers wag their tails like electric fans when they gallumph into the water and bring back sticks. Even when they're exhausted and hacking for breath. Why? Because that's what they were *born* to do. There, then, is the pivotal question that all the purely rationalist theories ignore: Where can we go in Quest for "Wow"? Where is the wonder that will resurrect us from apathy? What will make *us* wag our tails with joy, even when we're exhausted?

Provided, of course, we want to be happy rather than merely surviving.

Socrates, grandfather of Western philosophy, said that the crucial starting point in the quest to discover wisdom — "the purpose and meaning of life" — is the frank admission of our own ignorance. Because he was humble enough to admit he didn't possess wisdom, he was thus constantly in pursuit of it. He submitted to the inescapable truth that reality is simply too enormous to fit into our limited heads. As G. K. Chesterton argued, the chess player — the rationalist — tries to cross the infinite sea, thus making it finite. In contrast, the poet submits to the fact that the sea is infinite and revels in the endless possibilities. In the going, we're already "there."

For Confucius, "Humility is the solid foundation of all the virtues." Augustine believed humility is the first, second, and third most important factor in religion. Francis de Sales wrote, "True humility is to see yourself as you are seen by God, not more than you are and not less than you are." Snoopy put it squarely: "Has it ever occurred to you that you might be wrong?"

Humility isn't timidity. Nor is it the self-abasement that passes for humility among poor souls who can't bring themselves to be proud even of their hard-won successes. The Greek word so often mistranslated as "pride" — as in "Pride goeth before the fall" and "Those whom the gods would smite, they first make proud" — is *hubris*. To a Greek, that wasn't legitimate self-esteem from doing one's best but vanity, arrogance, the insolence of Adam and Oedipus who no longer needed the gods and all the gratitude and limitations that submission to a Higher Power entail.

The word "humility" derives from *humus*, "earth," and a quite satisfactory capsulization might simply be: "down-to-earth," realistic, knowing who one is and where one fits into the cosmic scheme of things — "not more than you are and not less than you are" — neither king nor serf but, as Jesus implied, Peers of the Realm.

T. S. Eliot puts it nicely, describing Polonius in "Prufrock":

> No! I am not Prince Hamlet, nor was meant to be;
> Am an attendant lord, one that will do
> To swell a progress, start a scene or two,
> Advise the prince; no doubt, an easy tool,
> Deferential, glad to be of use,
> Politic, cautious, and meticulous;
> Full of high sentence, but a bit obtuse;
> At times, indeed, almost ridiculous —
> Almost, at times, the Fool.

Healthy seekers have the grace to laugh at themselves, to take themselves seriously, but not *too* seriously.

Enough to Make You Humble

Absolute certitude — in politics or religion or any other human search — is the enemy of truth. The great sin is certitude; the great virtue is doubt, because doubt is a clear admission that, even if there is no God, I myself am unequipped for the job. Doubt guards against smug, ill-considered foolishness. Doubt sends me off in search of better explanations than I've comforted myself with thus far. Certitude is for jihadists, kamikaze pilots, and high-school seniors.

Especially those of us who are well schooled need to be taken down a peg, convinced like Socrates that we are honestly still ignorant of so much. (That could be one of the reasons God allows suffering.) We can legitimately write "Finis" to the quest only with our final heartbeat.

There are more realities invisible to us than there are material objects we can contact with our senses — or even with our most powerful microscopes and telescopes. No need (yet) even to venture into aspects of singularly human life that scientism would scorn as irrelevant, like honor, integrity, yielding one's own betterment for the improvement of others. For now, just consider the elusively mysterious elements of the *material* world that we tell ourselves we more-or-less do understand, when we're honestly just pretending we do. Kidding yourself takes no great effort.

Without your awareness or input the human body has 35 million digestive glands to process food. Your stomach acids could dissolve razor blades in a week, so that your stomach needs a new lining every three days or so to guard itself from its own juices, which requires the stomach to regenerate a half-million cells every minute. Every seven years your entire skeleton has replaced itself. If the DNA of an average person were uncoiled and strung out in a continuous thread, it would reach the moon and back a hundred thousand times. Within our very selves, these endless, miraculous transformations are relentlessly taking place.

When I discovered that, I said, right out loud, "Wow!"

We can't see gravity, but we have to submit it's real. It limits the number of times we can walk off the Golden Gate Bridge. It gives things weight, makes them fall, holds us up, keeps us glued to earth, and maintains the moon at a respectable distance. Sub-atomic particles perform their endless tasks, everywhere from the most distant galaxy to the innermost chambers of our own brains, racing at 40,000 miles a second. (For the number-challenged, that's 14 million mph.) Catching an atom in flight is like try-ing to lasso the wind. And it's been going on everywhere for 14 billion years before we came along. And most of us in the temper-ate zones, as we sit in our chairs right now, are hurtling eastward at 750 mph — while at the same time revolving around the sun at 67,000 mph. The answer to the question "What's up?" actu-ally changes from instant to instant, and means diametrically the opposite for a Laplander and an Australian. All that whipping around is powered by the sun disgorging energy inexhaustibly. And there are a gazillion trillion suns out there. Yet we keep saying, "The sun went down."

Wow.

More, what we regard as "stiff" matter isn't solid at all, no matter what our eyes and fingertips tell us. Each rock-solid object is a "work in progress," shifting, vibrating, and whizzing about, without benefit of our awareness. And — get this — most of it is empty space! If you could blow up a hydrogen atom to the size of the Superdome, the nucleus would be a grain of salt on the floor and the electron would be a tiny piece of grit up around the roof — and the rest is "empty." But (as we'll see later) it's not really, really "empty" but bristling with potential. Like the space inside a womb. Sort of. Even if we don't understand it, we'll all yield to the belief that $E=mc^2$. We admit energy *is* mass times the speed of light (180,000 miles per second), squared. In fact, matter is — quite simply — gravitationally trapped light!

Wow.

Philosophers used to be mocked for discerning how many angels could dance on the head of a pin, but for a century the question has been focal for quantum physicists whose expertise is validated by cellphones, computers, and atomic bombs. They testify to countless quanta (energy "packets") in a single cell in an eyelash, giving form and substance to everything we see — and to so much that we can't possibly see. Einstein said, "For the rest of my life, I want to reflect on what light is." But most people's knowledge of (and interest in) the gratuitous gift of light is similar to our knowledge of the inner workings of our cars and computers. We see only the tiniest bit of the light spectrum, but it *is* there. At the short end, invisible radio signals are zipping all round us. Just flip a switch and prove they're actually there. Invisible microwaves cook for us, power iPods and radar. Infrared light operates TV remotes, heat lamps, and night vision goggles. Then there's the teeny-weeny band of light we're directly aware of that triggers and sustains life, that allows us to find our way to work and home again, powers our lasers, DVDs, and printers. The evidence for invisible ultraviolet light is sunburns, but it also kills microbes, sterilizes instruments, and nabs counterfeit bills. Invisible X-rays help us look inside people, finger airport bombers, and allow astronomers to locate whole worlds no telescope could come even close to. At the far end, invisible gamma rays can kill cancer cells.

Wow.

As recently as April 25, 1990, the Hubble Space Telescope has opened our eyes to light even Galileo could never have dreamed of, automatically opening up the cosmos we can now be aware of. It also exponentially expands the true background against which we judge ourselves. It has validated the presence of objects whose light has traveled 13 billion (13×10^9) years to arrive. Their sources came into existence when the universe was only about a billion years old, 7 billion years before the solar system more or less settled into its predictable waltz around its sun. It's perfectly possible that that source of light is no longer even "there" anymore. Closer by, the light from Proxima Centauri, the closest star to us after the sun, started toward us 4.2 light years ago. Even though, from our quite circumscribed point of view, "the stars come out at night," they're actually there all the time. It's just that the presence of the sun in daytime upstages them.

Beyond dispute, all of that is going on. Every second. Without our awareness.

Wow.

For a century, quantum physics has enabled those unafraid of open minds to juggle all sorts of incompatibles. The atom looks nothing like our consoling image of a tiny, predictable Newtonian solar system. An electron "is" sometimes a pellet, sometimes a wave, depending on your viewpoint. Thus, if you fired an electron at a hypothetical barrier with two holes, it could go through both holes at once. Or reappear on the other side without penetrating the barrier! In the final analysis, nature is made up not of isolated, discrete building blocks but rather patterns of energy (quanta) interrelating. We are made of stardust! Every paltry pebble is a pulsating multi-universe! Is the realest-real what we can see or what *is?*

Complementarity

Reductionism is a way of simplifying puzzlements to their most fundamental parts for easier understanding — and acceptance. To put it perhaps too simply, it argues that "the whole is no more than the sum of its parts." All well and good, say, for explaining a machine by analyzing its physical components but, as the first chapter argued, most of the truly important realities of our lives do not submit that readily to such a material simplification — not even, we will argue later, the universe itself. Dissection won't answer the crucial question of that woman whose little boy died of a cerebral hemorrhage.

As a result of the many factors we saw in the last chapter, everything — I mean, everything — was handily reduced to the status of a machine. Newton's comfortably predictable universe worked like a magnificent clock, and it was consoling to consider God as a benevolent and attentive Watchmaker. Oversimplifications of Darwin led to the conviction that humans were just more complex animals, who were more complex vegetables, which were more complex dirt. Followers of Freud reduced human confusions to childhood sexual disfunctions, and followers of Adler simplified them to struggles for power. All of those understandings are true — but not exclusively or absolutely true. Each of them leaves out too much objective evidence pertinent to an honest assessment of What Is.

Part of our attempt to simplify truth in order more easily to cope with life is the simplistic recourse to *dualism* — which divides everything into either/or, which in turn makes judgment so much less painful. "Ya gotta accentuate the positive, eliminate the negative, latch on to the affirmative. Don't mess with Mister In-Between." An action is *either* good *or* evil; a sin is mortal or venial; you're unreservedly with us, or you're the enemy. Flesh and spirit are in constant conflict, like religion and science, discrimination and naive acceptance. Men are from Mars; women are from Venus. God is locked within the waterfall, or inaccessibly distant in heaven. God is a wrathful avenger or a Cosmic Pussycat. The elements of the Eucharist are Christ or bread and wine. The most pernicious reductionism is in the very definition accepted by even the most trustworthy of philosophers for human beings: rational animals.

To be humble, we have to accept that there are entities that seem undeniably *more* than just a sum of their parts. Like the negative and positive poles of a magnet, or a sperm and an ovum, which, joined, produce a new force neither has alone. Like the potential that comes into being by juxtaposing body and brain in specifically human animals: the soul.

It takes a certain courage to take up squatter's residence on one side or the other of any supposed dualism, but almost inevitably the result is out of kilter. At times painful. At times catastrophic. Human beings have been exterminated because they had the wrong color skin, the wrong shaped noses, the wrong beliefs.

The truth can never be at war with itself. We can't legitimately allow our preconceptions and theories — scientific or religious — to block out unwelcome truths. If the inner workings of subatomic realities can be explained only by denying that Newton's reliable laws governing macroscopic movements apply to them, then we have to go back — humbly — to the drawing board. If Galileo's meticulous observations prove conclusively that our planets move around the sun — and yet we also hold the Bible to be the word of its Creator, then we have to go back and harmonize the two so they both make sense, together. If the innermost hungers of specifically human nature universally yearn for a fulfillment neither the body nor the brain alone or simply adjacent to one another can satisfy, then science and religion have to start sharing notes.

One of the greatest obstacles to peace of mind and soul is the educated person's conviction that learning has been "settled" at the issuance of a diploma. A "terminal degree." The only reading now needed (beyond the commonplace and entertaining) is keeping up with our career fields. Our substantive learning may have settled into neutral, but enriching truths keep moving and multiplying. The sea is infinitely revitalizing itself — and it can do the same for us. There's far more available to life than just surviving it.

More to the purpose here, no matter what the ultimate cause of "Original Sin" — the solely human talent for botching up even the best situation — its effects are undeniable. It's the only "doctrine" you can prove from the daily newspapers. Whether there is a God or not, whether that weakness was inherited from our simian forebears or caused by some dumb human ancestor, human beings are capable of greater wickedness and degradation than any other species. Why?

Many notable thinkers like John Calvin, Voltaire, and Thomas Hobbes ("life is solitary, poor, nasty, brutish, and short") have accepted, at least in some degree, the idea that, because of the fall of our first parents, human nature in every possible aspect became totally corrupt and repellent to the Creator, and only through the infinite merits of Christ's sacrifice was God placated. Sort of. Not that the corruption disappeared, but that Christ's merits covered them like snow on a dunghill. It's a view many have found concretized in William Golding's *Lord of the Flies*. A group of pubescent boys, stranded on a desert island with no adult control, ever so gradually reveal the savage and murderous nature lurking beneath the veneer of civility that depended on stern adherence to law and order. Only cops can curb the inborn cruelty.

At the opposite extreme, others equally notable, like Jean-Jacques Rousseau, William Blake, and Walt Whitman, believed that human nature is innocent and corrupted only by the wickedness of cramping society. Children are filled with wonder, trust, and curiosity, incapable of wilfully harming others. It's a view embodied in J. D. Salinger's *A Catcher in the Rye*, in which all children are blissfully unsophisticated and genuine like Holden's brother, Allie, and sister, Phoebe, always in danger of the System turning them into "goddam phonies."

There is "justification" for either view right in the scriptures: "The Lord saw that the wickedness of humankind was great in the earth, and that every inclination of the thoughts of their hearts was only evil continually" (Gen. 6:5). And in the same book: "God saw everything that he had made, and indeed, it was very good" (Gen. 1:31).

Is the glass half full or half empty? Yes. Is an electron a pellet or a wave? Yes. Are human beings devils or angels? Yes.

The quantum Principle of Complementarity tolerates ambiguity, approximation, probability, paradox. Bipolar magnets and brains, the sexes, Trinity, symbiosis, Yin/Yang, transubstantiation. Not antagonisms but fertile togetherness, not indifferent potentiality but *eagerness* to be fruitful and multiply. Why pretend we understand what defies comprehension?

Today, the ideas available to ordinary people through the media and education range between two absolute extremes. At one end a technocracy that subordinates values to facts and at the opposite end a religious fundamentalism that suppresses facts in the name of values.

But the constitutive elements of all that exists are not either/or but both/and, more/less.

Can we be humble enough, no matter our ages, to admit that, although we've struggled all our lives to learn, what we don't know will always exceed — exponentially, endlessly — what we can grasp? As Hamlet told his learned academic friend, "There are more things in heaven and earth, Horatio, Than are dreamt of in your philosophy." There are levels of truth, meaning, complexity that escape the most astute and experienced observer. What would the brilliant author of Genesis make of Magellan's earth? Would Aristotle have appreciated Sartre? Could Newton have comprehended Heisenberg?

Can we be grown-up enough to surrender at least in part our hard-won knowledge and sophistication to regrasp the imagination, surprise, and wonder of children, in order to come at the Truth afresh? Can we approach the possibility that the universe is as much a self-expression of its Creator as the God who walked in the Garden with Adam and Eve and astonished Moses in the burning bush? Can we allow God to be not only a God of order, like the deist Watchmaker, but a God of surprises, the One who compacted *everything* into a dot smaller than a point in mathematics? For us to find him, we need not just the critical powers of intellect but the intuitive receptivity of children, a tolerance for ambiguity, a joy in the unending quest.

There is a lifetime of difference between our governing attitude if we look at our life in this universe as a tantalizing gift or as just ... "there."

Plunge humbly into the endless sea, and come up spewing *joie de vivre!*

THREE

Owning a Self

For what will it profit you
to gain the whole world
and forfeit your soul?
Or what shall you give in return
for your very self?
> — MATTHEW 16:26

We've grown used to speak of the "soul" as if it were an object, something we "have," like an appendix. It's that mechanical metaphor again. Even if we admit the soul's importance (like having "heart"), we still try to *locate* it the way neuroscientists try to establish what folds of the brain govern memory or movement. For that reason, many respectable scientists and thinkers believe they've debunked the very existence of a soul.

Probably no one who's read this far is an atheist. But, almost certainly, if your life seems "wowless," if you feel dispirited — enervated, listless, aimless — five'll getcha ten you've forgotten your soul, slipped into feeling it will take care of itself. Wrong. No matter what you claim, is it just possible you've been treating your "soul" no differently from the way an atheist would?

The great Nietzsche wrote, "Body am I entirely, and nothing else, and soul is only a word for something about the body." Paul Churchland, who holds the Valtz Chair of Philosophy at UC San Diego, asserts that there is "neither need, nor room to fit any nonphysical substance or properties into our theoretical account of ourselves. We are creatures of matter." Sir Cyril Bart declared,

"The chemistry of the brain generates consciousness as the liver generates bile."

Even Freud was co-opted by psychologists trying to establish psychotherapy as a "legitimate" (i.e., palatable to intellectuals) science. In a *New Yorker* article (May 1, 1982), Bruno Bettelheim pointed out that students of Freud, especially Americans, purposely mistranslated key terms Freud used, effectively turning an introspective psychology into a behavioral one. Purely left-brain psychology not only clung to unbending objectivity but succumbed to it, making the person an object dominated by "mechanisms" and a therapist a sophisticated mechanic — or at best a personal trainer.

Freud himself, however, wrote in "Postscript to 'The Question of Lay Analysis'": "Psychoanalysis is not a medical specialty. . . . I want to entrust it to a profession that doesn't yet exist, a profession of secular ministers of souls."

Freud was smart. Being human and being religious are two quite separable relationships.

Freud was a meticulous stylist. When he meant "soul" he wrote *Seele*. The word that the translators substitute for "of the soul" — "mental" — has an exact German equivalent; namely, *geistig*, which means "of the mind," or "of the intellect." If Freud had meant *geistig*, he would have written *geistig*. Bettelheim wrote:

> Freud shunned arcane technical terms whenever he could, not just because using them was bad style but also because the essence of psychoanalysis is to make the unknown known, to make hidden ideas accessible to common understanding. . . . Freud chose words that are among the first words used by every German child.

Freud didn't use highbrow classical words for what he believed were the major components of *die Seele*; he didn't label them the Id (the animal nature always ineradicable within us), the Superego (the rules uncritically taped as children) , and the Ego (the autonomous self), but *das Es* (the It), *das Überich* (the Over-Me), and *das Ich* (the Me). French translators render them *le ça, le surmoi, le moi*. The English translations convert them into an objective, cold, clinical relationship rather than a warm, personal, intuitive one. And the objective meanings are what filter down from the ivory tower to the graduate schools and thence to the Sunday supplements.

Freud uses "soul" as the overarching entity that encapsulates all the other functions: Me, It, Over-Me, conscious, and unconscious. He is not talking merely of mind, the intellect, but the whole *self.* What holds "the whole thing" together, cosmic and comic, paradoxes and all.

The crucial insight is that I don't *have* a soul. I *am* a soul. I have a body, which is surely a constitutive part of myself and influences me all the time, but it's a part of me I hope and trust I'll outlive — simply because the inner core of me is immaterial, not subject to the second law of thermodynamics that insists even granite is in the process of decaying. There is no annihilation, only transformation. Anyone who was ever privileged to witness the instant of a person's death knows that whatever served as the source of integral aliveness before is now incontestably gone.

"Soul" reflects the core of one's personal existence: the whole living being of an individual. But there are aspects of that reality that are often used as synonyms yet at least can be considered and better understood as separate facets of the one reality: spirit (a unifying vitality), character (conscience), and personality (ingrained habits of adapting).

"Spirit" reflects a *quality* of soul: the soul awakened (as Buddha means "the fully awakened one"). It is the "energy" we can substitute for "spirit" throughout the scriptures. It is an aliveness of the soul-self, as in "spirited," like the relation of the flame to the candle. Spirit is an energy that fuses the contrary facets within our selves as well as connecting our selves with those around us and with the universe. When the spirit is pulsing, we have verve, ardor, vivacity. We are *super*-natural! As St. Irenaeus said, "The glory of God is humanity, *fully alive!*" It is this spirit that has never been ignited in so many dead-ended eyes.

Neglect of the spirit is the death of Wow.

A single father wrote me about picking up his five-year-old son from summer camp:

> Yesterday after a full day of camp in the scorching heat, I picked up an exhausted lad, who, dragging himself over to the car, saw a tennis ball across the field, and immediately sprinted over to get it — heat and exhaustion ignored. Passion. It was way too hot for me to run, of course, and I was wearing wingtips, and I had avoided being sweaty thus far. . . . So I raced him! It's a great thing that being a kid is still as much fun as it always was, if not always so easy.

Why is it life is so exciting, till maybe the second grade, when the SATs start looming? When discovery becomes a monitored "task," and imagination is an obstacle, and all the magic goes out of just simply being alive? Could it be just possible to get that exuberance back?

Unfortunately, when our formal education ceases (and, too often, long before) we're just too *busy* to apprehend our own selves! We rarely take time to experience our spirits, even to feel that inner self as a unified entity, much less assume ownership of it, even less challenge it to greater aliveness. Liturgy rarely triggers it, not unless you have an *intense* faith before you show up. Rather, our selves are too often mixtum-gatherums, unopened rooms stuffed with conflicting desires, values, ideals, pulling us this way, then that. Similarly with conscience. Most of our "principles" are really only the contradictory clutter packed into the Over-Me (Superego), taped uncritically from all sorts of confounding sources. Character can *alter* personality. The rambunctious can become reflective, and the shy can become assertive. But only with conscious effort. That's why it happens so seldom.

Paradoxically, we're all alike, as humans, yet each of us is unique, as a self. Each of us has gone through the same stages of growth humans have gone through since the caves: birth, weaning, play years, schooling, adolescence, young adulthood, adulthood. And if we live, we also face inevitable aging and death. Thus, we can learn something about being human from every story in which we immerse ourselves, whether a modern novel or an ancient saga. Yet as individuals each of us is irreducible, even identical twins who are still two separate psyches, two intertwined but separate stories.

And there is a third aspect to the self, not only is each of us human and a self, but each of us is also a *participant*. Except for a few hermits, we are each part of a family, a community, a work force, a nation, and the whole human family. As Robert Kennedy once said:

> Each time a person stands up for an ideal, or acts to improve the lot of others . . . he sends forth a tiny ripple of hope, and crossing each other from a million different centers of energy and daring, those ripples build a current that can sweep down the mightiest walls of oppression and resistance.

Or we can actually oppose that evolution — merely by being lumps in its way.

Therefore we have three questions: What does it mean to be fulfilled as a human being? Who am I as a unique person? How do I fit into the web of relationships that is society?

In all three senses — human, self, participant — we are forever incomplete, on the way. A humanly fulfilled soul isn't a goal, but a process. Ideals, like the North Star, are guides, not a destination. We want not a static definition of self (like a textbook or a personality profile) but an ongoing, centered *sense* of self. Being a self should be *exciting!* Each of us is not only a fact but an opportunity. The song "Fame" says it: "I'm gonna *live* till I die!"

Being Human and Acting Humanly

There is one sure-fire test of any being's humanity, even one unborn: Does the entity have demonstrably, unarguably human parents? Debate closed.

But being human is no assurance of acting humanly. All other natures we're aware of — without exception — are inescapably programmed. No hungry tiger can refuse meat, no cabbage uproots itself for greener pastures, no rock decides to end it all and implodes. In marked contrast, humans are free to act like beasts, to vegetate, to treat others as stepping stones — or to be Abraham Lincoln, Florence Nightingale, Helen Keller, Albert Schweitzer. We're the only species forced to choices and decisions; thus, all education should be empowering us to reason and decide honestly and wisely. Anything less is merely Gradgrind job certification.

The Greek word for "soul" is *psyche,* which means literally "butterfly." It's an apt metaphor. By rights, the soul should emerge from the fusion of body and mind as naturally, effortlessly, gradually, and irresistibly as a butterfly easing bright-winged from within the ugly cocoon. But that's the human difference. We can refuse to emerge from the state of being merely rational animals. We can stay secure within the cocoon and die as human beings.

Today, tragically, the media seduce the young to adult ways before they have the slightest skills for personal discernment, before they can think honestly and choose prudently for themselves. The result is an ugly Too-Much-Too-Soon, captured indelibly by Nikos Kazantzakis's Zorba. His parable is worth quoting at length.

I remember one morning when I discovered a cocoon in the back of a tree just as a butterfly was making a hole in its case and preparing to come out. I waited a while, but it was too long appearing and I was impatient. I bent over it and breathed on it to warm it. I warmed it as quickly as I could and the miracle began to happen before my eyes, faster than life. The case opened; the butterfly started slowly crawling out, and I shall never forget my horror when I saw how its wings were folded back and crumpled; the wretched butterfly tried with its whole trembling body to unfold them. Bending over it, I tried to help it with my breath, in vain.

It needed to be hatched out patiently and the unfolding of the wings should be a gradual process in the sun. Now it was too late. My breath had forced the butterfly to appear all crumpled, before its time. It struggled desperately and, a few seconds later, died in the palm of my hand.

That little body is, I do believe, the greatest weight I have on my conscience. For I realize today that it is a mortal sin to violate the great laws of nature. We should not hurry, we should not be impatient, but we should confidently obey the eternal rhythm.

Who can reflect on that story without flashes of pretty little girls like Jon Benet Ramsey tricked out like seductive burlesque queens, middle-school girls with short-shorts and pierced belly buttons, fourteen-year-old boys asking, "What you say about sex doesn't count for oral sex, does it?" Think of the tabloids' darlings — pampered starlets, athletes, and rappers — thrust into wealth and privileged lives not even royal heirs could be prepared for, but utterly incapable of handling them without greedy managers. Or drugs. Or suicide. No one home inside. The *New Yorker* had a great cartoon of a little boy, clutching his teddy on the sofa between his parents, and saying, "During the next commercial, I'll have some questions about erectile dysfunction." If Booth Tarkington wrote *Seventeen* today, he'd have to call it *Ten*.

Human You

What will make humans "wag their tails" with joy, even when they're overwhelmed and exhausted? "What the hell are people *for*?" What understanding of "happiness" can survive years of setbacks, constant repression, the bleak agony of concentration camps? As we've seen and will see, there are lots and lots of systems that promise fulfillment. They do that simply by transforming an enticing, dehumanizing vice into a life-giving virtue. The American Dream makes a virtue of greed; the more things you have, the happier you'll be. The *Playboy* mystique and sit-coms make self-indulgence the key; life is to party! Warped experience of schooling (vs. education) makes mediocrity desirable; beating the system starts very early. Equally warped experience of "church" (vs. religion, a personal connection) can, quite naively, try to make the next world more important than this one. Peer and parent pressures make conformity a virtue, so that you want to "be somebody" — as long as you can stay exactly the same as everybody else.

Simplistic answers are always false. The foolproof test is the kind of people their devotees become. Human beings are too complex to be boxed in by half-truths, and individual humans are even more slippery to pin down — like trying to pinch mercury. No one is merely a head or a body or a heart.

There are two contrary tests of fulfillment. One is positive: What makes us proud, even when we're not feeling particularly jolly? The other is negative: What makes us grouchy, touchy, snotty day in, day out, hating work and life, like the man who couldn't surrender the fifteen grand? Hand it to Nietzsche: "Whoever has a *why* to live for can endure just about any *how*."

Another approach is to look at all other creatures (as God asked Adam to do at the start of the very first quest). "What have I got, that they ain't got?" With inanimate matter we share mass, weight, electrical charge, and an internal universe pulsating with energy and incessant change. With vegetative life we share a quantum leap upward from inert mass: the ability to take in food, grow, reproduce, mutate — but also a susceptibility to death. With other animals we share an incredible transformative leap up: the ability to move about, sense danger, feel affection, exhilaration, and pain. But as far as we know (so far), we're the only entities who have all those qualities together *plus* the ability to reflect and grasp that we *are* selves.

Learning and loving. Other animals can know *facts*; a stag pursued by hunters knows that there is danger. But as far as we can tell, it doesn't ask *why?* We not only can apprehend facts, but we also have the incredible potential to try to make *sense* of them, to *understand.* Other animals can give their lives to save their own, but only we can give our lives (often without dying) even for people we don't *like.* Further, no lion can become more leonine, no cabbage more nutritive, no rock more granitic. But "humanity" is a spectrum that ranges from pimps, pushers, and hitmen at one end (just over the line from beasts) all the way through most of us to truly exemplary humans like Joan of Arc, Shakespeare, Gandhi, Dorothy Day, Churchill.

Further, again as far as we know, no shark gobbles up a swimmer and plunges to the ocean depths uttering, "Oh, God! I did it *again!* I need counseling!" The shark was only "doin' what comes natcherly." Only humans suffer pangs of conscience.

And humans have another defining, constitutive potential. Even the toughest of us have succumbed to it: a placid lake with the moon lancing a silver scar across its surface, a beach assaulted by a storm, a summer sky whose fire-folk began their journey to earth before there was an earth. Changing musical tones and pulses of rhythm can move the heart and bring tears to the eyes. All those oh-my-God moments. Philosophers call that a sense of the *numinous* — an awareness of a *presence* beyond the sensibility of any receptor but the human soul. If God exists, that's who it is. And without a sense of that numinous aspect of our context, we are lessened as human beings. That is the answer to Peggy Lee's question: "Is that all there is?" No. It's not!

It's as if two contrary powers — flesh and intellect — are fused, like the positive and negative poles of a magnet, to generate a new third power: the force-field of the human spirit.

We can understand. We can love unselfishly. We can transcend ourselves till we die. And unless we make the effort to do that, we will never know Wow.

The specifically human hunger to learn can be placated by gossip, the ball scores, Trivial Pursuit. The specifically human hunger to love can be mollified by infatuations, idol-worship, masturbation, casual sex. The specifically human hunger to transcend ourselves can be numbed by body-building, portfolio building, empire building. Nothing wrong with any of those. Except they're not *enough*. Like junk food, their only result is momentary pseudo-satiety. And flab.

As A. A. wisely counsels, "Progress, not perfection." Perfectionism is blasphemous because, if there is a God, only God can be perfect.

However, that ineradicable hankering for perfection — to know conclusively, to love without fear of loss, to reach beyond our fingertips — just might be an intriguing clue that we humans are, by our very nature, made for a way of existing that extends far beyond this one.

Unique You

Your DNA code is absolutely one-of-a-kind. Even a flawlessly executed clone couldn't reduplicate all your *sui generis* experiences since that sperm joined that ovum.

A bit of reflection (probably best done on paper) can provide a preliminary sketch of the elements that would enable someone to pick you out of a line-up: sex, race, coloring, face, body, grooming. How you feel about sports, food, music, math — all the adjectives and adverbs that "modify" you, set you apart from the pack. If you're completely honest with yourself (on a retreat, with a counselor or therapist, in confession), you've begun to know how you feel about work, sex, love, learning, cheating, lying, trusting, and where you honestly need to challenge yourself. You should have at least begun "to see yourself as you are seen by God, not more than you are and not less than you are."

Oprah Winfrey, born on a dirt-poor pig farm in Kosciusko, Mississippi, writes, "Don't complain about what you don't have. Use what you've got. To do less than your best is a sin. Every single one of us has the power of greatness, because greatness is determined by service — to yourself and to others." What's standing between you and Wow is you.

Stop with incessant examinations of conscience! Instead, in honest humility list the assets you do have that nobody else seems to have in the same way or to the same degree. Then what?

Each of us is free to do absolutely anything we choose — accepting, of course, the in-built consequences. You're free to walk off the Empire State Building. But only once. You're free to treat gin like ginger ale and sex like double-solitaire. But not without a price. It seems human beings are made to use anything in the universe insofar as it makes us grow as knowing, loving beings, and to reject the use of anything in the universe that makes us less open to know and love. Such use of things to dehumanize or degrade ourselves or others would be morally evil — since "moral" means acting like a human and treating others as human.

Ironically, to be free *costs*. First, it requires that you ask the unnerving solely human question: Why? Then expend considerable effort to decide the reasons for and against any serious choice for you as an individual. Then you have to *commit* yourself to one choice — based on, at best, probability. And freedom (paradoxically) ties you down. In choosing one option, you automatically reject all the others — at least for a while. But the only alternative to the burden of freedom is slavery and victimhood:

Surrendering your freedom — your self, your soul — to some-one else. Dostoevsky's Grand Inquisitor says there's no gift that human beings will surrender more willingly than their freedom. If that's true, then there's no gift that human beings will surrender more willingly than their humanity and individuality.

Genuine freedom means the capacity to go *against* what "every-body knows, everybody says, everybody does." If you fail to choose to be a unique "Me," by that very fact you have opted to be a witless sheep. You can change at any time, but every day the probability dwindles.

Participant You

The Golden Rule — "Do unto others as you would have others do unto you" — is not a Christian monopoly. It's embedded in every life-giving philosophy ever conjured up (see C. S. Lewis, *The Abolition of Man*, "Appendix"). It's not a matter of religion but of human survival.

At times, being cramped together with other equally imperfect people — with their contrary agendas, infuriating habits, obstinate resistance — is a wearying burden. There are times when every-thing inside cries out, "Leave me *alone!*" But an instant's thought shows we surely don't mean that. One of the worst punishments imaginable is solitary confinement for very long. On the contrary, as Helen Keller discovered so dramatically, the absolutely most liberating realization is: "I'm not alone!"

What's more, we can accomplish much more together, pooling our various talents and making up for one another's deficien-cies. The impetuosity of the fiery progressive is balanced by the irritating hesitation of the cautious conservative. The sharp deci-siveness of the rationalist begs for the adaptive easements of the intuitive. Some are better at loading the cannons than at calling the shots. The best question you can ask is, "Here's what I'm pretty good at. How can I help?"

There is a profound difference between a congregation (*grex* = "herd") and a community (*unio*="connection"). The differences are obvious between, on the one hand, passengers on a bus, the ordinary classroom, an assembly line, and on the other an office party, a family picnic, a wake. A congregation is an accidental gathering of strangers with a common practical purpose; a community is a group of people who are unafraid of one another, vulnerable enough to accept one another's foibles and weaknesses, and unafraid to let their own shortcomings show.

It's a toss-up whether any formal religious gathering is a congregation or a community.

If each "participant" is teflon-cocooned even from the members of his or her own blood family, even a celebrant with the combined talents of Carol Burnett and Fulton Sheen is not going to raise the dead like Ezekiel with his field of dry bones. Nor is anyone going to commune either humanly or divinely if the defensive force-fields are on full charge.

Therefore, we have come upon yet another constituent factor in becoming fully human: vulnerability. The animal nature we share with beasts is relentlessly attentive to danger, constantly on guard. But our human nature calls us to evolve further than mere survival.

How does one "sell" vulnerability — the crucial component of love, faith, commitment, persistence, human and individual growth — in a world grown fearful of any risk without worry-free, money-back warranties? How do parents (who warn children not to talk to strangers long after they can ride the bus alone) help kids to be especially attentive to the unattractive needy? How do they inculcate the empathy that resonates with their pain and the kindness that brings compassion into their faces and voices and fingertips? I honestly don't know. But I do know that, without those sensitivities, Jesus Christ doesn't stand a chance.

He describes the only question at the last judgment to discern whether your human life was even worth living: "I was hungry,

I was thirsty. I was the one they called 'loser,' 'slut,' 'fag,' 'nerd.' What did you do about that?"

St. Paul offers the best revenge: "If your enemies are hungry, feed them; if they are thirsty, give them to drink; for by doing this you will heap burning coals on their heads" (Rom. 12:20).

The eccentric hero of *God Bless You, Mr. Rosewater* by Kurt Vonnegut Jr. is asked to give babies just one commandment to live by. He hesitates but then he says, "There's only one rule that I know of, babies. 'God damn it, you've got to be kind.' "

FOUR

Belonging

There's no place like home.
There's no place like home.
There's no place like home.
— Dorothy Gale

When a child wakes alone in the dark, she's lost in a featureless Dali landscape. So she cries out. Quick as electricity, her mother's there, flicking on the light, rocking her, and saying, "It's okay, honey. Everything's just fine now." At that moment, the mother is a high priestess of myth and meaning. Everything in the child's world has settled back "into place," as it should be.

No matter what our age, each of us still needs some matrix of meaning to hang on to, a background perspective against which everything can be measured so that it "makes sense." At least in the few moments we consecrate to getting our bearings, we need to feel, "It's okay, honey. Everything's just fine now."

I wonder if the reason we're so seldom ambushed by *joie de vivre* is that we're so vigilantly on guard against anything unpleasant that our defenses can't be penetrated even by joy! As Burger, the psychiatrist in *Ordinary People,* says: "If you can't feel pain . . . you won't feel anything else either. You know what I'm saying?" How can we feel joy when we've grown used to living on the defensive even against inconvenience? We're so occupied locking the windows and checking the alarm systems to feel "at home" anywhere. Even at home. For our first nine months we were as near to Eden/Nirvana/Heaven as we'll ever be in this life: warm, fed, floating, secure, without a care because we couldn't think.

But then, through no fault of our own, we were ejected out into the cold and the noise (just like Adam and Eve), and we received the first of what would become a lifelong succession of slaps to make us cry. (Without that pain, we'd have died.) As soon as possible, the attendants had to clean the infant and put her back next to that heartbeat that had been her assurance for the last nine months.

Then for about a year and a half, the parents (one hopes) try to get the infant to feel as close to the serene security of the womb as they can. Every cry and twitch is a signal for service. No matter how inconvenient, the parents' function is to respond. But after a while, again through no fault of the baby, the potential for muscle control activates, and parents have to begin to offer the next of that lifelong series of unwelcome challenges. (And even the most saintly have long since ceased to delight in changing diapers and cleaning up messes.) The child begins to hear two words she's never heard before: "Yes" and "No." The emergence of the Over-Me, so the child can learn to protect herself. The words themselves are meaningless, but after a while the smiles and frowns of the food-suppliers convey the intent well enough.

As we've seen, every woman and man since the caves has faced those same unwelcome, jarring separations: weaning and potty-training, being pushed out to play, schooling in the skills of the tribe, the godawful upheaval of adolescence, falling in love, separation from the shared story of the birth family. Each one forces an *alienation* from dependable parents, purposefully, so that at each stage we can be just a bit more independent, able to survive on our own. *Hansel and Gretel* teaches that children have to be forced from the nest to learn how to live by their own wits and imaginations. All the unpleasant disconnections have a life-enhancing purpose.

Folktales — stories societies have told for centuries — are background maps to explain growing up. The heroine or hero is forced from home on a perilous journey or some displacement (like a new wicked stepmother, i.e., Mom being human). This has made "home" not the same source of reassurance it had always been. It's in all great myths and parables: the *Odyssey* and the *Aeneid*, the uprootings of Adam and Eve, Abraham and Sarah, Noah, Rachel, the missions of Buddha, Jesus, Paul, and Mohammed, *The Divine Comedy*, *Pilgrim's Progress*, *Gone with the Wind*.

Yet even if the journey lies away from home, the goal is always to return home. As Dorothy says when she clicks her red slippers, "There's no place like home." But she returns to Kansas not the dismissible girl she was; she is now becoming a woman. The same holds for Frodo Baggins, Luke Skywalker, and Harry Potter. The goal of the evolving soul is personally to bring cosmos out of chaos again (just as God did), but it will not be the old order but a new, different, better one. A hard-won, *personal* sense of belonging. That's what adolescence is *for*.

Precisely by rising to the challenges of her adventures in Oz, Dorothy discovers that the magic in the ruby slippers is herself.

Without conscious effort and a resolute decision, we forget as we grow older that life isn't a state we struggle to survive in, but a Quest.

A Meaningful Myth

> All vagrants think they're on a quest. At least at first.
> — John Updike

What separates travelers from vagabonds is having a map and a destination.

Similarly, our estimate of our physical proportions is impossible without external gauges. In a telephone booth (if such still exist), even a small person has recognizable height. Next to the Sears Tower, the individual shrinks drastically. Imagine someone on a map of the United States, and their significance becomes meaning-less. Extend the background even to the temporary limits of the Hubble telescope, and an individual becomes less than a sneeze in a hurricane.

However, there's no need to go so physically far. The crucial determinant of our ultimate meaning is just down the road a piece: the fact of unavoidable death. Does whatever background we find truthful give us a sense of value, a motive to keep going, even if our days are also constrained by our share of time coming to an end?

Do I matter? Am I useful? Have I value? We need some coherent, consistent context against which to justify the struggle and assuage our fear of futility. Many words designate the background story or map against which we judge our value, meaning, purpose, progress. "A philosophy of life," "a myth," "a meaning-system," "a core belief," "spirituality," "religion." We need to discover a *pattern* to life in the muddled elements of our experience, with a basis for hope, so our very being isn't haphazard. The activity of a beehive or assembly line may be purposeful, but it's not meaning-ful. They have market value, but no *inherent* human value.

Meaning, value, purpose, and commitment are inseparable. Without them, there's no hope of coherence or fulfillment in an individual's life. For those who "keep their options open," life is merely something that happens to them: One-Damn-Thing-After-Another. Without a coherent story-line, life "is a tale told by an idiot, full of sound and fury, signifying nothing."

But we use the words "meaning" and "myth" as if we really understood them, when their content is actually a pair of blurs we'd be hard-pressed to explain to someone else.

"Meaning" can denote both *intention* (as in "I didn't mean to hurt you") or *significance* or *importance* (as in "Why worry about something so meaningless?") Here, we intend both senses: (1) Intention: Is there Somebody who purposefully allowed me to live, programmed into my very nature an objective for me to fulfill so that I can be satisfied with my life? If not, I have to arbitrarily choose some goal to occupy myself till death conclusively limits my freedom. (2) Significance: Against the background of the perhaps-infinite universe and the intimate intrusion of death, do I even *matter?* If there is a provident Creator who knows my name and cares for me as a person, He/She/They bestow importance on me. Barring that, however, I'm left to concoct some transitory value for myself until the mortician arrives.

"Myth" has two valid but contradictory meanings, as different as "false" and "true." The more usual meaning is a commonly held delusion, like the myth that the earth is flat or that handling toads causes warts. The opposite meaning — as in the Myth of Sisyphus, or the Grail, or Willy Loman — is a story that acts like a universal symbol, trying to capture a truth about life in a metaphorical way rather than in a rational way. The difference between a myth and a philosophical or theological system is that, in a story, you can get inside the hero's skin and walk around in it a while. You can *feel* their insights, without their scars. It's the reason to read novels. These myths last because they embody a universal truth that penetrates all times and cultures. In this positive sense, all religions and philosophies were meaning-laden myths before they became the rational systems most of us were limited to by our pragmatic, death-to-Wow schooling.

The psychiatrist Viktor Frankl, who survived the severest belief-test in history in the Nazi camps, called spirituality/myth-making/philosophies "man's search for meaning." Sigmund Freud had said the patterns of our lives could be explained by contending with sexuality. Alfred Adler insisted it was motivated by trying to overcome an inferiority complex. But Frankl saw that those who kept their sanity in the camps were those who had some *reason to keep going.*

He quotes Nietzsche's dictum: "Whoever has a *why* to live for can endure almost any *how.*" Human beings can keep any degradation at arm's length, if they can cling to a value within the soul: a loved one, an unfinished project, a purposeful cause, a provident God. A map.

> We who lived in concentration camps can remember the men who walked through the huts comforting others, giving away their last piece of bread. They may have been few in number, but they offer sufficient proof that everything can be taken from a man but one thing: the last of the human freedoms — to choose one's attitude in any given set of circumstances, to choose one's own way.

One's freely chosen myth/philosophy/religion will ground one's attitude to *everything*.

Value / Purpose

However, as we've already seen, pragmatic modern society isn't exactly eager to reflect on spirit or spirituality. Today's ethos is hard-nosed, street-wise, skeptical of "The Big Picture." Who thinks of living a noble life now when the *National Enquirer* has made heroes an endangered species? To a great many, the very ideas about spirituality are outlandish, like Madonna's Kabbala, Tom Cruise's Scientology, Richard Gere's Buddhism — or at the other extreme sheerly emotional like televangelism. Nowadays, other than "love," there's no reality more bastardized and degraded than "value."

As we saw before, the best-selling author Richard Dawkins insists our "obsession with purpose" is a "nearly universal delusion." But if it is in fact "nearly universal," how can we disregard that drive from our understanding of being human? How deadly dull it is to endure a completely purpose-*less* activity — like being on hold for twenty minutes, being stuck in traffic, proctoring study halls. If Dawkins is right, and we have no more future than ants or bees, if the rock Sisyphus endlessly shoulders up the mountain will — predictably — roll back down, give me a reason just to keep *going?* Then maybe we can talk about being happy!

Who can discern a difference between inherent value and market value in what Terry Eagleton describes as "a world bleached of inner significance"?

Ask any student in high school, college, or grad school: "Why do you submit to this? What is the value of 'getting an education'?" I'd wager, almost without exception, every one (and their parents) would reflexively answer, "You need it to get a good (i.e., well-paying) job."

That is, of course, patently false. No one needs trig to balance a budget or irregular French verbs to operate a first-rate bistro. Moreover, granted in a simpler era, Abraham Lincoln, Sojourner Truth, Harriet Tubman, Thomas Edison, Mark Twain, and Henry Ford had no formal education at all beyond perhaps a bit of grade school. Dave (Wendy's) Thomas, Ray (McDonald's) Kroc, Christina Aguilera, Peter Jennings, John Cheever, and Frank Sinatra never finished high school, but have lived in pretty high tax brackets. Walter Cronkite, F. Scott Fitzgerald, Robert Redford, Steven Spielberg, Tom Hanks, and Clint Eastwood never finished college. Eugene O'Neill, John Steinbeck, and Ernest Hemingway never finished college, but all three managed to win the Nobel Prize for Literature. William Faulkner won it without finishing high school. *Bill Gates* never finished college.

All you need to be materially successful are the four D's: discipline, drive, determination, and a dream. And the dream motivates the other three. But I know of no institution from grade school to grad school that teaches those, except by happenstance.

In the interest of efficiency, our schooling (vs. education) is divide-and-conquer. Each department has its restricted specialists, so that no student need realize that math logic and verbal logic are exactly the same process with different symbols, or that human sex is more than just knowing the crude mechanics. They need

never sense every "subject" is focusing on exactly the same questions: Who are we and where do we fit in to all this? They can be
effectively trained to make a living without ever asking what the
hell living is for. They scorn wiser people who use the words "sort
of" and "maybe" a lot. They make notes only of what's spelled out
on the board, if that. "Will this be on the test?" Since all human
questions are reduced to problems, they need never find an incentive — an *attitude* — to keep going when, as Chesterton wrote, "I
tell thee naught for thy desire save that the sky grows darker and
the sea rises higher." Well done, Gradgrind.

Pundits lament that the percentage of students prepared for
college-level reading peaked at 55 percent in 1999 and has declined
since. In 2001, 46 percent of students in the California State
University system's twenty-three schools needed remedial English classes. Since almost all students today are computer literate
and touch-type, they equate writing with keyboarding. It seems
unavoidable that those who don't have the skills to write an outline
lack the skills to think for themselves.

And for the nonreflective, there are plenty of quick-fix myths
that offer a spurious shape and form to One-Damn-Thing-After-
Another. Each separate sport, the "music scene," soap operas,
films, business — just like formal religions — all have their tribal
loyalties and rivalries, rituals, legends, iconic heroes, battles, spectacular events, joy and agony. They have their scriptures and
homilies, cathedrals and suicidal saints. (Look at any check-out
line in the developed world.) All opiates for the people. Just like
the Nazi Nuremberg rallies. At their most pernicious, you find
Jim Jones of Jonestown, David Koresh of Waco, Marshall Apple-
white of Hale-Bopp. At their mildest, merely quirky, like Shirley
MacLaine.

Still, they fulfill a profound need, a deep sense of belonging and
personal validation.

Who needs the effort and discipline to find a personal ortho-
doxy? People who think.

In the nearly half-century I've taught high school seniors, it has never failed that one didn't ask, "Why are you telling us all this stuff? Why can't we just enjoy being ordinary?"

Because life won't let you. Not when "things" go terribly wrong, when you need a motive just to keep on trying.

Unless education is the process of finding one's own meaningful map, we spend all those years giving them the skills to play volleyball. Then we send them out into a minefield.

Choosing to Be Important

The most incomprehensible thing about the world is that it is comprehensible.   — Albert Einstein

The crucial test of any myth is whether it copes satisfactorily with the one life-factor that's beyond argument: death. Death poses an iron dichotomy: Either we go on, in some unforeseeable manner, or we simply stop being real. We can forget any dodges like "falling asleep" or the Greeks' Hades or the Hebrews' Sheol where we go on "somehow" but are unaware of it. We can forget reincarnation since, if I am the survivor of a streetwalker who passed on in the early morning of August 18, 1931, her experiences are lost to me and therefore meaningless.

There are only two alternatives: we continue or we cease. If there's no afterlife, whoever has a flat EKG has stopped existing, like a computer file in a power outage. Pffft!

Atheism is much bleaker than most of those who claim it realize. Death doesn't just end the pain. From the only point of view that counts — my own — it's "the total End of the World." All the struggles to maintain integrity, to act nobly, to keep learning become unimportant. That bleak stance may seem justified to a college student who's never truly suffered, but it simply won't "work" standing next to the coffin of your mother or your child. If the universe is simply "there," uncaused by a purposeful Creator, then it serves whatever purpose we arbitrarily, temporarily assign to it. Then pffft! Our ingrained demand for reasons is a curse, because there are *no* reasons. By the mere fact of being born (for which we weren't responsible), we're summarily condemned to death. Life is an Easter egg hunt, and there are no Easter eggs. In the end, Helen Keller and Hitler get the same treatment: annihilation. It makes no difference whatsoever which map and attitude you chose.

Nonetheless, atheism is a quite defensible life-view. Very few have claimed to have gone through death and come back to testify that it's transitory. Just as many have claimed to have been wafted off in UFOs. The truth — which most catechism and religious ed and theology classes never broached — is that we don't *know* whether we go on or stop. No matter how convinced the professor or teacher — and we — were back then, belief or disbelief in a transcendent dimension to human life is still a *bet*, a calculated risk, one way or the other. That's what "faith" *means.*

On the one hand, the reality of undeserved suffering alone is enough to convince many clear thinkers to reject a purposeful Creator out of hand. His inefficiency and wastefulness in taking so long to get to humans is another argument. Forget the story of Noah; there have been at least five major extinctions just in the last 500 million years, which annihilated 60 percent of marine life, dinosaurs, and other gigantic reptiles.

On the other hand, as Einstein wrote, the very comprehensibility of the universe — the four predictable, controlling, and inescapable *laws* of gravity, electromagnetism, and the two nuclear forces — seem evidence enough of a Lawgiver, a Mind Behind It All. In accepting the Nobel Prize for Physics in 1918, Max Planck said, "We must assume behind this force the existence of a conscious and intelligent mind. This mind is the matrix of all matter."

Therefore, perhaps the most basic choice a human can make — an attitude that will govern every other life-choice — is: Am I prepared to *bet* on being meaningful or meaningless?

Blaise Pascal (1623–62), a mathematician who invented the first mechanical calculator and had no fondness for Jesuits, posed the human question with crystal simplicity: "God is, or he is not." One *or* the other. God can't sort-of exist, any more than we can be sort-of dead. The crux is that it is utterly impossible to be absolutely certain which is the truth. So, Pascal argued, since it must be one or the other, and since one is appealing and the other is appalling, I might as well choose the appealing one. I can spend my one life assuring myself that everything does in fact make sense and will work out, or lamenting that everything I struggle for is so much potential garbage. If I choose the appalling option, I face a grim life of trying to survive even though survival is ultimately futile. If I choose the appealing option, I'll never discover I was wrong.

If the undeniable yearning to have some personal meaning and value, as Dawkins insists, is a "nearly universal delusion," why is it so persistent? And why does it remain "nearly universal"? What is the good of "survival of the fittest" when I myself simply won't survive?

If there is a provident Creator who knows my name and cares for me as a person, He/She/They bestow importance on me. If not, pffft! God. Or Nothing. No other choice.

The Cosmic Context

A human being is a part of a whole, called by us "universe," a part limited in time and space. He experiences himself, his thoughts and feelings as something separated from the rest . . . a kind of optical delusion of his consciousness. This delusion is a kind of prison for us, restricting us to our personal desires and to affection for a few persons nearest to us. Our task must be to free ourselves from this prison by widening our circle of compassion to embrace all living creatures and the whole of nature in its beauty.   — Albert Einstein

In a monograph (2010), *Expanding the Spiritual Exercises* (of Ignatius Loyola), Roger Haight, S.J., argues that the scope of spirituality for the lifetime believer ought to be amplified, at both ends, regarding both our origins and our destination. So much has been discovered about our "background" since Ignatius wrote in 1541, and since the time most practicing believers set aside formal religious training. As a result, our awareness of our overall context is still to all intents little different from a medieval peasant's, with heaven still "up there" and hell still "down there," as if we really believed that the sun rises and sets. Attempting to have some kind of adult sense of God, the Bible, ourselves, our origins, and our future, with what we "sort of" learned back in college or even high school, is grievous self-impoverishment. Not including the valid insights of Darwin, Einstein, Jung, Bohr, Bultmann, Hubble, Rudolf Otto, William James, the Leakeys — yes, even of atheists like Christopher Hitchens and Richard Dawkins — is like restricting our minds to the thirteenth-century knowledge of Aquinas and imagination of Dante. We limit our understanding of the focal factors of our existence and our value (and values) to the capacities of children. Without the innocence.

Unbeknownst to the authors of Genesis, the universe took quite a bit longer to form than seven days, in fact, nearly 14 billion years. Despite their understandable ignorance, the earth was a gigantic sphere, which nonetheless shriveled in size in contrast to its Milky Way Galaxy, which is 100,000 light-years in diameter — and a fairly small neighborhood at that compared to the endless, endless galaxies stretching outward practically to forever. Beneath their very feet, there were fossils 600 million years old. Contrary to their firmest B.C.E. convictions — which lasted well into the nineteenth century — they shared a common ancestor with chimpanzees.

Most of us have been apprised that the universe is expanding, but few, I suspect, have had the time (or perhaps even the inclination) to wonder what effect such an insight would have on our

background map of What Is. The prophet Jonah was so intimi-
dated by God's request to convert pagan Nineveh, which was so
huge it took three days just to cross through it, that he ran in the
opposite direction toward Spain. But if (without a caring God) we
seem puny next to the Sears Tower, what purpose and significance
do we have if the universe is really 14 billion years old, and at best
we'll each last only eighty years, and our cozy Milky Way would
take about 100,000 years to cross? What is our "context" if our
background is nearly endless and still *growing?*

In fact, it can be one more new insight to re-ignite our wonder!

Brian Swimme has a delightful down-to-earth explanation of
the expanding universe we share. He asks the reader to imagine being inside a loaf of in-process raisin bread, perched securely
on one of the very many raisins called Earth. We are "inside the
cosmic process" which has been "rising" for 14 billion years.

> You will see that all the other raisins are moving away from
> you as the bread bakes, so that in terms of the bread's expan-
> sion you find yourself at the very center. And anyone else on
> another raisin throughout the loaf would come to a similar
> conclusion — hence, we have in this raisin loaf a model for
> an omnicentric reality. ("Up" has no meaning except from
> the point where the observer happens to be.)
>
> But there's more. Suppose you now try to determine
> whether or not you and your raisin are moving with respect
> to the bread [*the universe*] itself. What you will find of course
> is that you're frozen in place, for your raisin sits *stationary*
> with respect to the surrounding bread. And when you think
> about it a bit you realize that the very reason the raisins
> are moving away from you is because of the expansion of
> the bread. You and your raisin are not even moving; it's the
> space in between the raisins that is growing larger.

Isn't that delightfully confusing? But is it any less enlightening,
more flummoxing than:

We believe in one God, the Father, the Almighty,
maker of heaven and earth, of all that is seen and unseen.
We believe in one Lord, Jesus Christ, the only Son of God,
eternally begotten of the Father,
God from God, Light from Light, true God from true God,
begotten, not made, one in Being with the Father.
Through him all things were made. . . .

And we've professed that, publicly, since we were children. Week after week. For quite some time, we've at least *claimed* that those words of the Nicene Creed are our map, our myth.

Are there many of us, without advanced theological degrees, confident enough to explain what "all that is seen and unseen" now includes? How the Father and Son can both be God, "one in Being," or the difference between "birthed" and "begotten," especially before there was sex? Does it trouble anyone that heaven is not an "up" that the Son could come "down" from? Is it really as important as we were told that Jesus' mother was virginal? What probative evidence could you personally offer for the resurrection of Jesus? And your own? And these "scriptures" we always thought were dependably guaranteed by an all-knowing God. Haven't you heard even your kids saying they're taught that the Bible is just a bunch of made-up stories? Myths, in the "false" sense? If Jesus "ascended" from Palestine where does an old Australian lady rise to? And if we know, by definition, that heaven — where God dwells — had to antedate time and space, how does the Father have a right hand? And if we will enter heaven bodily, does it make any difference, really, how a body can exist where nothing is material — as long as we do get "there"?

More, are feminists somehow "wrong" to argue that the Holy Spirit is a way of describing the "feminine" in God? Are women weaker members of the "one, holy, catholic, and apostolic Church"? "One baptism for the forgiveness of sins." Does that mean that when we hold a child at the font, we have to accept (against every other inclination) that this little being who can't control his own excretion is a "sack of inherited sin"? As for that, what can we say for our well-intentioned Protestant friends, our Jewish golf partners, our atheist bosses? If any of our children cease worshiping, will they descend into the fires of hell when they die? Does your sincere belief in "the resurrection of the dead, and the life of the world to come" genuinely lessen your anguish at a loved one's wake?

Also, except for baptism, there's nothing in there about the sacraments, even Eucharist. Nothing about the hierarchy, or even priesthood, much less its limitation to males. Not a word about birth control or war or capital punishment or abortion or economics. Not a hint about punishment. Are all those packed into "Church"?

To repeat: Is our awareness of our overall context to all intents little different from a medieval peasant's, with heaven still "up there" and hell still "down there," as if we still believed that the sun rises and sets?

One thing for sure, in contrast to a child's universe presided over by a grim, bearded personage on a fiery throne, with a big book on his knees the Everywhere God is a lot more fun!

F I V E

The Everywhere God

If I go up to the heavens, you are there;
if I make my bed in the depths, you are there.
— PSALM 139:8

Ignatius Loyola popularized a lead-in to prayer (connecting to God) called "Composition of Place," in which he suggested we use all the senses approaching a scripture passage — open up a space in our imaginations to encounter God person-to-Person, embodied in Christ. For instance, before sauntering into the Sermon on the Mount (Matt. 5:7), close out all distractions and feel the chalky dust between your toes, the sweat adhering your feet to your sandals; sense the burlappy prickle of your only tunic; smell the acrid sweat of the other disciples; focus beyond the other heads on the face and body of Jesus — not the blue-eyed European of so much art, but a swarthy, brawny Jew with carpenter's fingers. If you put yourself close enough, you can smell him, too.

If you make that effort, you'll find it much more intimidating to hear him say, looking you straight in the eyes: "*You* are the light of the world." It's up to you to brighten the lives of others. Even your own life will have no exuberance unless you yourself ignite it. Just as the magic in the ruby slippers was Dorothy, you *are* the Wow!

On retreat, I find it helpful each year to use that method while meditating on Jesus washing the disciples' feet, looking up from my knees at the faces of those I work and live with every day, pondering as I move from one to the next my willingness and my reluctance. "Of course, I'll wash your feet. It's a privilege."

Then scrunching over to the next: "Well, . . . okay." But then after another scrunch, I look up and say, "I'll *die* first." In such a place, it's less possible to kid yourself about your virtue.

Far easier to engage a this-world God in tangible Gospel scenes like that, however, than to relate person-to-Person to the transcendent God who we also profess is omnipresent. Not the puritan Micromanager of childlike credulity who's "gonna find out who's naughty and nice." Nor the dewy-eyed Jesus of our cowboy hymns who just wants us to "be not afraid" and leave the driving to him. The One we mean when we say "We believe in God, the Father Almighty."

Something exhilarating could happen to your living if you ever owned the truth that the Unspeakably Holy One, the Architect of infinite quasars and infinitesimal quanta — the Ultimate Wow — knows your name, calls you his, finds you precious. Gasp!

Something vital got lost on the pilgrimage from Vatican II. Mercifully, the fires of hell dwindled; we dethroned the Dickensian Moneylender cataloguing every peccadillo; we discarded our ace of trump, fear. But in the process of humanizing a feudal worldview, we also traded the sometimes majestic organ for well-intentioned guitars, esoteric Latin for uninspired pap, Bach for imitation-Bacharach. Beyond the bland liturgy, our overall purview gradually twisted from a clutter of bloodless canonical strictures on our choices to even paler Hallmark do-good-ism. Few grow nostalgic for vengeful patriarchy, but we are left with restless hearts. Quite likely, such softness led to what now seems the full flood of efforts by so many devoted people to "reform the reforms," to get back to the "good old days," which really weren't that terribly good.

What did get lost on the trek was the transcendent God.

We miss the *Mysterium Tremendum* of Rudolf Otto, the Power thundering at Job from the whirlwind: "Where were *you* when I laid the foundations of the earth?" Moses described that Force as a blazing bush that did not consume itself; Isaiah cringed and tried (inadequately) to capture this stupefying Act of Love as an enthroned Personage ablaze with light, around whom an incandescent hurricane of voices swirls, shouting, "Holy! Holy!"

Such immensity tempts one to resign one's intelligence like Eastern mystics before the impenetrable Ultimate — before whom all words fail, even "is." Western theologians effectively stifled the awe of the theophanies — person-to-Person encounters with the eternal deity — which had always been the core of all religions before the rational Greeks came along.

If bishops wonder why "they're not coming to church," there's the reason: they don't find there a personal *connection* to that enthralling God — which is what "religion" means. No wonder.

Oddly, the physical sciences, once believed more antithetical to God than Freemasonry, can actually exorcise our exhausting rational attempts to box in this horrific Energy. Physics can help us return to a hazier, whirling, exhilarating awareness and friendship with God, childlike Christmas-expectancy, an awareness of God so many have lost to sophistication and more pressing demands since the end of formal schooling. Instead of trying to wrestle God into rigid formulas as our schooling tried to do, we can learn to *dance* with him!

Today, all but rigidly atheist scientists are humbler than many of us were led to believe. They speak not of inflexible certitudes as religions do but of hypotheses always yearning for improvement. Their insights into the way God made the universe can enrich our belief and our connection to that energizing Power more profoundly than stories that intrigued the first readers of Genesis — and perhaps ourselves when we were more credulous. In the past, secular science's "dangerous" insights into symbols, languages, and other cultures revitalized our knowledge of scripture, albeit at the price of complacent literalism, unquestioning dogmatism, and stern uniformity of belief and reserved practice.

The quantum view is bewildering, but no more daunting than Trinity, Transubstantiation, or Trent. Simply substitute "Energy" for "Spirit" in scripture and *feel* the faith-difference!

Perhaps science and religion could tease one another to look at our common reality from the other's privileged perspective. What if, against science's near-certain conviction, there *were* a Light faster than light? (Einstein spoke of the speed of light *squared!*) So fast it's everywhere at once. Like God. So hyper-energized it's at rest. Like God. And now scientists believe that when they crack the ultimate kernel they'll find nonextended energy. Like God. Couple that (despite previous mutual isolation) with God's response (Exod. 3:14) when Moses asked God's name — his role in reality: *Ehyeh asher ehyeh* — "I am who am, the pool of existence out of which everything draws its 'is'!" He is "the love that binds everything together in perfect harmony" (Col. 3:14).

What if, rather than remaining "outside" his creation like a deistic Watchmaker, the Creator embedded himself *into* that Singularity within which the entire expanse and power of this universe were compacted just before the Big Bang — tinier than the power of Beethoven once embedded in an invisible fertilized ovum? Just as the inescapable laws of gravity, electromagnetism, and the strong and weak nuclear forces are encoded right into "the way things are" from the outset, why not also the longing for life, feeling, and intelligence? God not merely as observer but participant! What if Divinity fused himself *into* creation before the start — just as many of us believe He/She/They later focused into Jesus of Nazareth? If ordinary folks are temples of the Spirit, why not the entire universe? *Matter never was completely inert!* Such insight could render moot creationist and intelligent-design explanations of how God had to step in occasionally to inject powers he had mistakenly overlooked, like self-replication (growth), feeling, movement without outside impetus, and consciousness.

Unlike the anthropomorphic Creator (of all beliefs), this God felt no need for immediacy or efficiency. He dallied serenely for periods inconceivably long to us, perhaps because he took such delight in just *being,* in watching stories emerge once he had invented time. Mary dared to say, "My soul *magnifies* the Lord"

(Luke 1:46). Similarly, Jesus says his whole purpose was not that we survive, unbad, but that we "have life *more* abundantly" (John 10:10). St. Irenaeus said the glory of God is humankind *fully* alive. Could such privileged souls be wrong when they imply that the God so clearly infatuated with evolution is *involved in it himself?* It seems heretical. The great Teresa of Avila felt it: "The feeling remains that God is on a journey, too." Would a God who *grows* necessarily imply prior imperfection (to anyone but a rationalist)? But what if it were true, that — like a child out of time, who has never aged — God finds delight in discovery more tantalizing than static certitude?

In 1932, Heisenberg won the Nobel Prize for the Principle of Uncertainty, maintaining that in the subatomic world the consoling predictability of Newtonian physics applies only "sort-of." The best one has in predicting activity there is "high probability" — which any human already knew was true about settling on a career, choosing a mate, having children, boarding a subway unarmed. Every act of faith is a calculated risk. Even the Thomists of Vatican I, who declared under anathema we can know God with certainty, accepted three *degrees* of certainty: absolute, physical, and moral (i.e., high probability).

As we saw before, nature is made up not of isolated, discrete building blocks but rather patterns of energy (quanta) interrelating. Singing "We are one in the Spirit (Divine Energy)" is not just a bromide metaphor!

"In the beginning was the Word, and the Word was with God, and the Word was God" (John 1:1). The Greek term for that Eternal Entity is *Logos*. Its connotations are abstract, cool, depersonalized, clinical, erudite, and mechanized — in short, "scientific," like the intellectualizing of Freud. That is the God most students encounter still, totally different from the tangible, personable, this-world Jesus. In contrast, the Aramaic for that same Divine Entity is *dabhar*, which Diarmuid O'Murchu insists is best translated as "an irresistible creative energy exploding into prodigious creativity." That understanding is closer to fecund primeval swamps than to the cultivated groves of academe. Such insight doesn't deny rational theology, but it suggests that our adult idea of the Almighty and our religious connection are severely impoverished without the corrective of its (seemingly incompatible) opposite. This is not an abstraction but the *living* God.

Maker ... of All That Is Seen and Unseen

> In the beginning when God began to create the heavens and the earth, the earth was a formless void and darkness covered the face of the deep, while the spirit of God swept over the face of the waters.   — Genesis 1:1–2

Since most of us put formal education aside, "all that is seen and unseen" has skyrocketed geometrically. If the accumulated knowledge of humankind up to 1900 doubled by 1950, that cumulus doubled again by 1960. By now, what we don't know redoubles just about every hour!

That extraterrestrial "deep" (void, abyss, "a soup of nothingness") has to be separated from the unsophisticated cosmology of the first Genesis writer. Clearly, there couldn't have been "heavens" or "earth" or "waters" yet, since God is just beginning to bring them forth. According to the Genesis writer, there isn't yet any light or even any suns to generate it. (But one has to admire a thinker twenty-five hundred years ago with the insight that everything initially came out of water.) So before there was anything else, there was the void — nothing. Except a God who antedated everything material and temporal.

Modern physics can enlighten us here, too. Their belief now is that the "condition" before the Big Bang was a "vacuum," not a mere emptiness but a "yearning for fruition," at least remotely analogous to a womb. As Brian Swimme explains it: "If all the individual things in the universe were to evaporate, one would be left with an infinity of pure generative power." Stretching from the empty space between superclusters of stars to the gaps between the neurons in our brains, there is a constant explosion and reconfiguring, birth-death-resurrection. From our limited point of view, like fireflies on a summer night. Despite our resolute conviction that "reality" can mean only "material things," what seems merely inert matter is *vitalized.* As Teilhard de Chardin wrote, all creation is "impregnated by His potent influx." And again, "Without any doubt, there is something which links material energy and spiritual energy together and makes them a continuity. In the last resort there must be but one single energy active in the world." Even St. Paul spoke of Christ as "all in all" (Eph. 1:23).

The physics of relativity flies in the face of Descartes' inflexible rationalist dualism that divides all reality into the physical (*res extensa*) and the cerebral (*res cogitans*), which infiltrated our own learning without criticism at so many cracks and crannies. Relativity asks us to understand instead that the observer is an integral part of what it is observed. With even a thin understanding of contemporary biology, one becomes aware that one's own self is part of a vast, living ecology, a web of living organisms, each distinct but inextricably conjoined.

The divine will to life inebriates all reality.

A wisdom that transcends our own has been guiding things for billions of years before we arrived. That same Spirit who hovered over the primeval waters, that infused itself into the primal combustion, that uses the four aboriginal laws of physics to guide every twitch from within everything with "is," is the same Spirit-Energy-Power who ignited the burning bush, who hovered over *all* the disciples (not just the priests), whom we ingenuously claim to have received into ourselves at baptism and confirmation. (Do you really *believe* that?)

Miriam Winter expresses that cosmic cohesion:

Everywhere we choose to go, we walk on holy ground. The soul of the universe is divinity present everywhere and in everything, in you and me, in friend and foe, in all who share our sacred space on our hallowed planet.

We've heard the same insight since we were children:

For I was hungry and you gave me food, I was thirsty and you gave me something to drink, I was a stranger and you welcomed me, I was naked and you gave me clothing, I was sick and you took care of me, I was in prison and you visited me. (Matt. 25:35–36)

Mystics are gifted to see the unity in chaos. So are quantum physicists.

God Unbound

Genuine science — physical, psychological, theological — must humbly accept that *any* of our formulaic traps cripple the mercurial Truth they try to encompass. All sciences must submit to the Truth rather than trying to dominate Him/Her/Them.

The quantum principle of complementarity — which most of our training either ignored or scorned — tolerates ambiguity, approximation, probability, paradox. It "allows" life to be far more mercurial, fascinating, invigorating, rather than chock-full of well-filed, sterile certitudes.

The God no scriptural writer was able to contemplate is present — vibrating, enlivening, urging further — everywhere within the universe. Despite our certitudes, matter is not basically solid. $E=mc^2$ *means* energy (E) is the same as mass (m) times (c) the speed-of-light, squared. "I am the pool of existence out of which everything draws its 'is.'"

This is not pantheism, which postulates God has no identity apart from the universe. St. Gregory of Nyssa wrote: "When one considers the universe, can anyone be so simpleminded as not to believe that the Divine is present in everything, pervading, embracing, and penetrating it?" Hildegard of Bingen heard: "Mine is the mysterious force of all that lives — I, the fiery power."

William Blake wrote:

> To see a World in a Grain of Sand
> And a Heaven in a Wild Flower
> Hold Infinity in the palm of your hand
> And Eternity in an hour.

And Hopkins:

> The world is charged with the grandeur of God.
>   It will flame out, like shining from shook foil...
>   nature is never spent;
>   There lives the dearest freshness deep down things;
> And though the last lights off the black West went
>   Oh, morning, at the brown brink eastward, springs —
> Because the Holy Ghost over the bent
>   World broods with warm breast and with ah! bright wings.

And e. e. cummings:

> i thank You God for most this amazing
> day: for the leaping greenly spirits of trees
> and a blue true dream of sky; and for everything
> which is natural which is infinite which is yes
>
> (i who have died am alive again today,
> and this is the sun's birthday; this is the birth
> day of life and love and wings: and of the gay
> great happening illimitably earth)
>
> how should tasting touching hearing seeing
> breathing any-lifted from the no

of all nothing-human merely being
doubt unimaginable You?

(now the ears of my ears awake and
now the eyes of my eyes are opened)

This is not a textbook God but the God whom Complementarity accepts can be eternal, omniscient, a fearsome Energy — and yet closer to us than our own heartbeats.

Imagine feeling that at Mass.

Spirituality is, as Viktor Frankl put it, "man's search for meaning." We are the only species whose choices are not branded into the fibers of our natures. We must *choose* to be who we are. But first we must discern what human beings are *for.* And we have only two backgrounds against which to measure our worth. Our lives are either speckles of light against infinite darkness or smudges of gray within infinite Light. We are here to discover our shining (Matt. 5:14).

Liturgies that make the community as important as its Host miss a crucial truth. We ought not limit ourselves to a companionable fellowship with the Good Shepherd. We are also "connected" into an Inexhaustible Energy whose infusion ought to make us recognizably more alive the rest of our week than those who ignore Him/Her/Them.

SIX

Jesus for Adults

I have come to bring fire on the earth,
and how I wish it were already kindled!
— LUKE 12:49

The apostles Peter, James, and John were twice privileged above the others. According to the Gospels, only those three saw Jesus at his most exalted other-worldliness and also at his most degraded this-worldliness. Only they were taken aside from the rest to witness Jesus transfigured (Matt. 17:7) and Jesus gripped in a terror so agonizing he sweated blood (Luke 22:44).

Our Christian education faithfully inculcated in us the dogma that Jesus was, to believers, undeniably *both* transcendent and immanent, completely divine and completely human. He was, on the one hand, the intimidatingly exalted Being we saw in the last chapter, but he was also the Jewish peasant born in a cold stable, who trained and sweated as a workman, and who was flogged to the bone before his ignominious death. But — somehow — our well-meaning teachers, no matter how lofty their credentials, seemed at pains to keep the two aspects of Jesus as distant from one another as the cerebral Greek and gut Hebrew mentality, the rational and intuitive intelligences, the stereotyped dominating "masculine" and the submissive "feminine."

I can't recall any theology professor ever telling us he prayed.

And that hardly seems changed. The learned lectures still focus almost exclusively on Jesus' natures: Just how did the Father "beget" the Son so that "they" were the same true God? If such rarefied questions in the Creed trouble readers, I direct them else-where, since I have never found any explanation either needful or available or, in fact, possible. "For our salvation" will come later with "for our sake he was crucified." Nor do I believe many today are anxious about the Virgin Birth. Aware as we are now of ways in which fallible humans can effect conception, it should cause no disquiet to admit that the One who readily brought a universe out of nothing could quicken an ovum in any way He/She/They had a mind to.

Probably more dominant in our ordinary lives than formal the-ology, the consoling weekly homilies and cowboy hymns seem intent only on the Jesus who cherishes, short-shrifting the Jesus who challenges. All in all, even now, he still seems offered as a model for good little boys and girls, someone who'd never embar-rass the family, never cause a fuss, never venture out of line. In that regard, the Lamb of God seems to have devoured the Lion of Judah.

Another opening for complementarity: "fruitful togetherness."

Became Man

"The Word *became* flesh" (John 1:14). The doctrine of the incar-nation (embodiment) is a *crucial* Christian doctrine. Without it, Jesus was no more one of us than a Hindu avatar come slum-ming among humans. Without it, Jesus is no possible example for fault-laden, doubt-ridden beings. Without it, only a sham "body," donned like a coverall or a disguise, perished and returned, which offers little hope for those of us entirely enmeshed in real bodies.

Somehow (who could dare say how?) the almighty Creator, who blasted Nothing into Everything, who profligately populated the universe with astonishing galaxies, who ignited life and intelli-gence and spirit — this *limitless* God freely constrained himself to the limits of humanity: doubt, desertion, derision, and death. Became the weakest being we know, a human infant.

Who, though he was in the form of God,
did not regard equality with God
as something to be exploited,
but emptied himself,
taking the form of a slave,
being born in human likeness.
And being found in human form,
he humbled himself
and became obedient to the point of death —
even death on a cross.   — Philippians 2:6–8

Being Christian means accepting that the overwhelming celestial Personage of the last chapter once had dirty diapers someone else had to change.

The Son — the Word "through whom all things were made" — "emptied himself," gave up the divine foresight that well-meaning homilists insist on forcing back into him, as if he *knew* how everything would turn out. ("Oh, my little brothers and sisters! Our precious savior saw that wicked cross looming up before him, always!") That mindless generosity would deny Jesus' total humanity, since humans are the only creatures with the burdens of uncertainty and doubt. The Gospel claims that "Jesus *increased* in wisdom and in years, in stature, and in divine and human favor" (Luke 2:52). Further, retaining divine certainty would make Jesus' agony in the garden and near-despair on the cross hollow pretenses at humanity. He would have known with utter confidence that "everything is okay." In a more commonplace way, retaining divine certitude and objectivity would deny Jesus' genuine irritation at his friends' thick-headedness, which we share, but also deny his endless patience, which we can only struggle to share.

The human Jesus we find in the Gospels also defies the reductionism that restricts him to "I am meek and gentle of heart" (Matt. 11:29). The novelist and medieval scholar Dorothy Sayers

short-circuits that simplistic emasculation about as well as anyone I've read. Let this quite lengthy quote from her *Creed or Chaos*
put an end to "Jesus, the Warm Fuzzy," a savior for children who
have yet to face serious temptation and tragedy.

> The people who hanged Christ never, to do them justice,
> accused Him of being a bore; on the contrary, they thought
> Him too dynamic to be safe. It has been left for later genera-
> tions to muffle up that shattering personality and surround
> Him with an atmosphere of tedium. We have very efficiently
> pared the claws of the Lion of Judah, certified Him "meek
> and mild," and recommended Him as a fitting household
> pet for pale curates and pious old ladies.
>
> To those who knew Him, however, He in no way sug-
> gested a milk-and-water person; they objected to Him as
> a dangerous firebrand. True, He was tender to the unfor-
> tunate, patient with honest inquirers, and humble before
> Heaven; but He insulted respectable clergymen by calling
> them hypocrites; He referred to King Herod as "that fox";
> He went to parties in disreputable company and was looked
> upon as a "gluttonous man and a wine-bibber, a friend of
> publicans and sinners"; He assaulted indignant tradesmen
> and threw them and their belongings out of the Temple; He
> drove a coach-and-horses through a number of sacrosanct
> and hoary regulations; He cured diseases by any means that
> came handy, with a shocking casualness in the matter of
> other people's pigs and property; He showed no proper def-
> erence for wealth or social position; when confronted with
> neat dialectical traps, He displayed a paradoxical humor that
> affronted serious-minded people, and He retorted by asking
> disagreeably searching questions that could not be answered
> by rule of thumb. He was emphatically not a dull man in His
> human lifetime, and if He was God, there can be nothing
> dull about God either.

But He had "a daily beauty in His life that made us ugly," and officialdom felt that the established order of things would be more secure without Him. So they did away with God in the name of peace and quietness.

Salvation

For our sake he was crucified, died, and was buried.

Why?

In what follows, I don't deny the centuries' old doctrine of atonement. Forthrightly I do confess I find it totally repugnant in the light of the God Jesus revealed. I acknowledge with some apprehension that I take a position counter to the one strongly asserted by St. Paul, who said, "Therefore, just as sin came into the world through one man, and death came through sin, so death spread to all because all have sinned" (Rom. 5:12) and "You were bought with a price" (1 Cor. 6:20). I challenge also the great Father of the Church and saint, Augustine, who contended that original sin passed on from one generation to the next — via sexual intercourse! More recently, the new *Catechism* states: "Jesus atoned for our faults and made satisfaction for our sins to the Father" (615).

Even before Jesus, I believe on the solidest scholarship that the story of Adam and Eve is a symbolic fiction, that it tells in a parabolic ("curve-ball") way the undeniable truth that human beings, in even the most ideal situation, will find a way to screw it up. (I might be remotely open to a punishment of such magnitude for purposely annihilating 20 million Russians, 15 million Europeans, or 30 million Chinese, but not for one piece of "fruit." Not if God is wiser and kinder than I am.) Knowing what St. Paul was incapable of knowing, I'm also nearly absolutely certain no human being was the cause of death. We have all those dinosaur bones to substantiate that fact. It is unconscionable that God — who apparently knew what he was doing — could create us free and imperfect, then punish us for using freedom imperfectly. What's more, "ransom" is paid only to a *hostile* and unrelenting power. If God were in fact so implacably wrathful that he inflicted the "stain" of that primal sin on every infant born of the human race, refusing to forgive till Jesus "paid off" the debt, I find that flagrantly contradicts the countless centuries in which Yahweh remained steadfastly loyal and protective to the errant Hebrews. But most compelling of all, according to Jesus, the father of the prodigal son ran to the boy, embraced him, and kissed him *before* the kid uttered even a word of apology. All he had to do was show he wanted forgiveness. And the Jesus who revealed *that* insight about God also enjoined us to forgive one another seventy times seven times (Matt. 18:22). Surely, then, we can expect as much of God.

One is hard-pressed to find a vindictive God in that. This is, yet again, the easy-to-hand Economic Metaphor so quickly seized by those incapable of grasping or tolerating love without conditions or meriting. It's an explanation for people who value justice more than kindness, reparation more than forgiveness, obedience more than conviction, brains more than hearts.

Terry Eagleton seems to agree: "[Jesus'] Father is neither judge, patriarch, accuser or superego, but lover, friend, fellow-accused, and counsel for the defense. The biblical name for God as judge or accuser is Satan" (see Job).

Juxtaposing the unarguable human predilection for screwing up *and* what we know now about human evolution (which almost no one before *The Origin of Species* even suspected), I find it difficult enough to accept that an all-wise Creator was imprudent enough to give a cerebral cortex and freedom to an inadequately evolved tribe of apes, without having to fuse the Good Shepherd and Baal.

But I yield to the Spirit working in the Church, who allows that doctrine to persist. Nevertheless, I honestly confess I can't comprehend it.

Moreover, I believe there is an explanation beyond atonement.

A frighteningly bright little boy once provoked a better answer from me. He'd been to all the Holy Week services with his parents. But the following week he asked me, "Father, if God loved his Son so much, why would he make him go through such an awful, awful death?" He'd blindsided me by using the word "love" — which leaves no recourse to some pagan divine justice requiring sacrifice of a firstborn Son. The only answer I had for him is still the best I know: "To show us how it's done. With trust. With love. With dignity." At every step of his passion, Jesus showed us real courage, that is, fearful courage, the faith that says, "I *can't!* But I'll *try!*"

Can we accept the complementarity in this crashing contradiction? Here is the God we've already seen: the God who defies all words, formulas, and categories, the almighty Creator, who blasted Nothing into Everything, who profligately populated the universe with astonishing galaxies, who ignited life and intelligence and spirit — this *limitless* God compacted into this blood-crusted wretch?

The crucifix captures that sermon. It says, "Is *this* enough? Does *this* tell you how important you are to us, how trivial you let yourself become, how eager we are to forgive?"

I find no problem — in fact I gratefully accept — that Jesus' act of love is a treasure I can call on for sins I've committed myself, a gift without which I would feel helpless to apologize enough for by myself. I believe it to be given through the sacrament of reconciliation. But I shudder at accepting it as a result of "baptism for the forgiveness of sins" committed by two fictional characters, inflicted on us for the simple fault of being born human.

No child or adolescent could comprehend that Jesus or that God. Not without having "been there," lost in the apocalyptic emptiness of betrayal, worthlessness, near-despair. The mild Good Shepherd is for children. The Hero of Holy Week is for adults.

The great question is whether even adults can submit to *being* loved *that* much.

Jesus said, "I lay down my life for the sheep" (John 10:15). But what does our "salvation" mean? It can't mean, as students *still* maintain they've been told, that Jesus "saved us from sin and death." How do I know? Because people still sin and die. Haven't their teachers noticed?

Jesus' death saved us from the *fear* of sin and death — the self-loathing dread that our sins are beyond forgiveness and the atheist's bleak resignation that death negates everything we've tried to make of ourselves. Those two liberations seem more worthy of worship than emancipation from a debt to an unforgiving Bondsman that we weren't even alive to incur.

He Rose Again

If, as some learned authorities insist, the Gospels are a colossal hoax, the writers missed a superb opportunity to work up a scene to rival Peter Jackson and Steven Spielberg: "The face of the tomb began to tremble. Light speared out from the cracks. Suddenly, the rock blocking the entrance crashed down and Jesus strode forth, trailing light." That took less than two minutes.

But they were so naive that they didn't. How easy it would have been to fake an eyewitness — say, one of the Roman guards who saw the whole thing, converted, and conveniently died in battle someplace so he couldn't be questioned. In fact, besides showing the leaders of the operation at the very time they wrote as complete cowards and numbskulls, they described the whole pack of them sneering at the women who came to tell them the tomb was empty. And did you ever notice that whenever Jesus appeared, they didn't recognize him? Even after Jesus had supposedly told them he would rise? Even the three who had witnessed the transfiguration?

And yet St. Paul says, clearly, "If Christ has not been raised, your faith is futile" (1 Cor. 15:17). The same learned voices who believe Christianity a hoax also claim that, despite the fraud about divinity, Jesus was a good man and a wise counselor. Sorry. Jesus — and those who spread the word of his rebirth — didn't allow that condescension. He — and they — clearly asserted that Jesus was equal to God. Here are only a few examples, rendered all the more credible because they come from the hearts and minds of unwavering monotheistic Jews, who would never have trifled with such assertions or profited from them dishonestly, nor would they have gone to ghastly deaths rather than simply deny them and escape.

– "The Father and I are One." (John 10:30)

– "According to the flesh, comes the Messiah, who is over all, God blessed for ever." (Rom. 9:5)

– "Every tongue shall confess that Jesus Christ is Lord [i.e., Yahweh]." (1 Cor. 2:11)

– "For in him all the fullness of God was pleased to dwell, and through him God was pleased to reconcile to himself all things, whether on earth or in heaven, by making peace through the blood of his cross." (Col. 1:19–20)

– "All things came into being through him, and without him not one thing came into being." (John 1:3)

– "Thomas answered him, 'My Lord and my God.'" (John 20:28)

In Mark's Gospel, the first written life (ca. 65 C.E.), the entire structure of the book builds to the climactic moment when the high priest faces down Jesus with the critical question: "Are you the Messiah, the Son of the Blessed One [YHWH]?" (Mark 14:61). And Jesus answers with the unspeakable name: "I AM" — an allusion to the self-definition of Yahweh in his reply to Moses, "I am who am" (Exod. 3:14).

It's hardly likely that, in the actual historical situation, a monotheist like Thomas could have said those words only one week after the resurrection without fear of blasphemy. It took the best minds of the early Church over three hundred years to come to any reasoned conclusions about that boggling insight. Even we, who grew up from childhood with at least the *assertion* of Jesus' divinity/humanity, would be at a loss to explain it. But it is also undeniable that the earliest writers felt no hesitation to profess belief in it. The basis for Christian belief in the resurrection — and, thus, the very credibility of Jesus — is the shocking result the disciples' belief had on their behavior. In the first place, the thorough cowards of Holy Thursday and Good Friday, who fled their teacher and friend and hid behind locked doors for three days, defied all expectations. Less then two months later, on Pentecost, these misfits strode forth boasting of their experiences of the risen Christ, defying prison and death (Acts, passim). What's more, secular historians testify to the fact that many of them went to horrifying deaths rather than deny that experience. They could have lived if they'd only confessed it was a hoax. Every martyrdom was a deathbed confession.

There is the rock-bottom question and the rock-bottom testimony. Take it or leave it.

Ascended into Heaven

I had my first tailspin encounter with the inadequacy of the Creed back in May 1964, the year after I was ordained. I was slated to give a homily on Ascension Thursday. Even then, I was hyperaware of a congregation's boredom tolerance, so I wanted to give them something *new*.

If you discount all the paintings of the ascension (from artists of varying talents and unknown beliefs), there's very little to rely on in the New Testament. Matthew and John don't mention an ascension explicitly at all, and Mark's and Luke's Gospels hold it to one verse. The only "lengthy" treatment is in Luke's Acts, and after a farewell from Jesus, the ascension itself again rates only one verse (1:9), followed by two verses in which two men in white robes ask them what they're still hanging around for.

So I sat, as focused as I could be, and conjured an Ignatian composition of place. I was right there, in the scene: the dust, the heat, the stink of sweat — my heart and mind still befuddled with having spent over a month with a man who'd been certifiably dead. We're on a hill; Jesus says goodbye. Then he starts to rise. Very slowly. I focused intently on the moment till he had gotten about where most of the paintings freeze him: arms out, streaming light, serene.

Nothing new there.

So something (Someone?) nudged me into letting the scene continue. That's where the challenges came.

Jesus just kept rising, like a missile in low gear. Up, up, up. Then, the left side of my brain (where I stored all my knowledge of science) began an unaccustomed conversation with my right brain (where I had insulated my faith). "Did he go through the Van Allen Belt," the left-brain inquired, somewhat superciliously. "Was his 'glorified body' radioactive? Did it keep soaring through the nearly infinite cold of space and then come to the thin, thin membrane that separates the universe from heaven? And he went through it — *boop!* — like a self-sealing tire? And then he was home, striding through gates made of pearl along streets paved with gold, with angels whizzing all around, strumming their harps?" The left-brain didn't want to lose traction, so it pressed on: "While we're on this, where do they get oysters to make those gates, and where do they mine that gold, outside the universe, where nothing physical exists? Oh, yes, and if your Jesus went 'up' from Palestine to heaven, where does an Australian aborigine rise 'up' to?"

Back to the drawing board on that one.

Here I was, after a couple of years of twentieth-century physics, but my understanding and faith shackled to the cosmology of first- and fourth-century minds — no matter how holy and inspired. If both the disciples' experience of the risen Jesus *and* the cosmos that's now opened by scientists from Copernicus to Hubble are *both* true, then there must be some complementary way the two can coexist. In a world that can tolerate black holes (regions in space so dense nothing can emerge, even light), and worm holes in space (short-cut tunnels like a kind of umbilicus between two vastly separated galaxies), we may not have an easier time grasping what happened to the risen Jesus, but we really ought to have more subtle and supple imaginations to approach the task.

"Beam us up, Scotty!" Only the most primitive tribes alive today have not seen even one of the many *Star Treks* in which material bodies are "tele-transported" from some planet back into the *Enterprise*. Is that what happened to Jesus at the ascension and to us when we die? Probably not. But it's quite likely less taxing to us than a body rising through space in first gear.

Our attempts to evolve metaphors for transcendent realities try to physicalize entities we believe are real but aren't physical. Therefore, each one is necessarily inadequate. Just as the roses I give you as a sign of my love only *try* to stand for love, and the love doesn't die when the flowers die, so early centuries' attempts to grapple with otherworldly entities are not literally true, but better than nothing. Can I describe "red" to a blind man? Yes. Sort of. It's like the hot taste of cinnamon candy on your tongue. That's not it, but it's better than just sneering and denying it's possible. (How do rationalists cope with real love?)

There are no authentic travel guides to heaven and hell, but anyone has as much right to "solidify" them as Dante had. In "No Exit," Jean-Paul Sartre does a much better job with hell: a hotel room in which three people who detest one another have to spend eternity. (I can think of fifty people. . . .) In *The Great Divorce*, C. S. Lewis pictures hell and purgatory as the same "place." Not the intriguing punishments of Dante, but worse. A gray town where everybody is sullen, nasty, hate-filled. For anyone who surrenders self-absorption for humility and gratitude, their stay has been in purgatory; anyone who refuses goes back to hell, freely chosen rather than yielding.

Even slight consideration shows that, if we do go on, there *must* be some kind of "hell" for people who simply don't want to go "anywhere" where Someone Else is more important than they are. And there has to be a "purgatory" for those who are still too cautious, too uptight, too fearful of sanctions, too ill-prepared for joy. They have to accept that Christ *makes* them worthy.

If we agree that without an afterlife our specifically human yearnings would be curses, we have to resign ourselves humbly to accept that we do continue to live — "somehow" — and leave questions of our accommodations to our Host, who has more experience at that.

Yet again, modern science can help. It's now a given of physics that matter converts to energy, and that energy can't be destroyed. Iris Laine explains how we experience something at least remotely similar to our transformation at death every day in dealing with water. When the weather gets cold enough, it becomes tough enough to stand on. When it warms, those little particles start dancing so we can swim through it. Really heat it up and it becomes steam that can power great engines. If an electron can go through both holes at once — or even materialize on the other side of the barrier without penetrating it — God had already solved problems like ascension. (Too complex to compact here, but Google "Hyperspace" or "Action at a Distance" or "Bell's Theorem" and see all the bewildering fun-analogies the witnesses of Jesus' departure could have used.)

Eastern mystics believe that a spark of the divine Brahman lingers in every living being, and in Nirvana all that energy merges into the All. Mystic-scientists like Teilhard de Chardin believe our spirits are absorbed into that energy stream that is the earth's consciousness (the Noosphere) and are lovingly preserved — as selves — within God's eternal Now.

Is that the way it really is? Probably not. But it's better than nothing. Or Nothingness. And it beats hell out of the Baltimore Catechism!

As for the early Church writers' seeming lack of concern for the ascension, quite likely the reason was that, although Jesus had gone into another way-of-existing, he was still right there. That's what the Eucharist was all about.

To Judge

Here is an area that is perhaps the most critical for many — even many who left formal religious learning only recently. But it's surely a sticking-place especially for mature born-Catholics. Just as with our afterlife images, we become prisoners of our metaphors. The clear-cut, dualistic, judicial metaphor insists on either/or, mortal/venial, finely calibrated divisions — disdaining more/less, "sort of," and "I don't know enough to judge."

In our seminary courses in canon law, it at least seemed we were being trained to snoop out hidden crannies in confessions that would allow us to *withhold* absolution. Something primitive persists in the otherwise Christian imagination that still retains in our deepest psychic rooms the image of the scowling Bookkeeper sitting with ink-stained fingers at a huge book, just waiting to find reason to spill us off the tightrope into the bowels of hell. (Which has a lot more to do with the pernicious "Santa Claus Is Coming to Town" in Advent while we also "wait for Jesus" than parents may realize.)

It seems extremely reductionistic to believe that every less-than-human transgression must be either "mortal" (totally severing a connection to God) or "venial" (trivial and beneath concern). Even today, sophisticated teenagers are still obliquely asking, "How far can I go?" Does any friend ask a question like that?

Surely as with any person-to-person relationship, there is a whole spectrum of insults between the deadly and the insignificant. Can any follower of Jesus accept that, if a committed couple with children use artificial birth control even just once, it's the same as bombing an orphanage?

Jesus said just two commandments encompass *all* the expectations God has of us (Matt. 22:37–40): We love God by loving the neighbor. And he explained quite clearly and concretely how we do that in the story of the Good Samaritan (Luke 10:25–37) and in the one crucial question at the Last Judgment (Matt. 25: 31–46): "I was hungry, I was thirsty. . . . " Our fitness for heaven will not pivot on our wickedness but solely on our kindness.

And I make bold to suggest there are more insidious ways we withhold our kindness than the patent acts of selfishness we learned of when we were younger. There are challenges for Christian adults that probably weren't posed to "good little boys and girls, who'd never embarrass the family, never cause a fuss, never venture out of line." I don't recall anyone suggesting we were less than Christian when our shyness kept us "reserved," when our silence in the face of injustice signified consent, when we contented ourselves with being sheep rather than shepherds, when complacency secured us in stagnation, when perfectionism misled us into the hoary old sin of Adam and Eve.

Morality is about justice: living up to objective obligations rooted in our horizontal relationships with every human being and our vertical relationship to God. Following Christ goes much further; it's about love, which is very difficult for the self-absorbed to comprehend.

Real love isn't just a feeling; it's an act of will that takes over when the feelings fail, when the beloved's no longer even likable. When Jesus enjoins us, over and above justice, to "love our neighbors," he doesn't ask us to *like* them. He asks only that we give them respect, concern, tolerance, at times patience. Often he asks us to challenge the neighbor, to stand up to bullies, to offer "tough love." And he asks us to be solicitous for them, especially when we sense their need of healing. In our overcrowded, rushing world, it takes an effort merely to give the neighbor even our *awareness*. Passing by a beaten man in a ditch on the road to Jericho — or a drunk in a doorway — may not be unjust, but it is un-Christian.

In *Les Misérables*, when the gendarmes return Jean Valjean with the stolen silverware to Bishop Bienvenue ("Welcome"), the bishop tells them not only that he gave the silver to the thief but that he'd forgotten to take the silver candlesticks, too. That's not justice; it's Christianity.

And it's surprising how many baptized Christians, old and young, find that absurd.

Perhaps the greatest burden Christianity adds to the burden of being a good human being and a grateful child of God is that as we are forgiven we must forgive. It's a burden we incautiously accept every time we say the Lord's Prayer: "as we forgive those. . . . " The prodigal father sees the sinner from far off and runs to him and kisses him *before* he has a chance to apologize.

Justice (morality) requires that, once atonement has been made, the debt disappears. Christianity (love) requires that, even though one can demand restitution of the thief, the thief himself is forgiven before that. Jesus said it from the cross: "Father, forgive them. They do not know what they are doing" (Luke 23:34).

That commandment — to love God by forgiving the unlike-able neighbor — makes avoiding sexual temptations seem like child's play.

SEVEN

In Fulfillment of the Scriptures

Finally, beloved, whatever is true, whatever is honorable,
whatever is just, whatever is pure, whatever is pleasing,
whatever is commendable, if there is any excellence
and if there is anything worthy of praise —
think about these things.   — PHILIPPIANS 4:8

A good Jewish friend who is very well-read, astute, and a firm believer occasionally grumps to me, "You people [Christians] are constantly plundering our [Hebrew] scriptures trying to shore up your man's [Jesus'] claims. Well, we wrote them, and we don't think so!"

That's not at all what we were taught as we came along, but he's quite right. Recorded eyewitness testimony to the risen Jesus corroborates Christianity, or nothing does. Scriptures can become much more invigorating to the soul when we stop using them as just an arsenal to prove we're the toughest kids on the block and the only ones with the *really* right answers.

That defensive, apologetic, stiff-chinned preparation was (perhaps) warranted when we felt beleaguered by all those Protestants and Masons and freethinkers, but it ill befits anyone who has authentic faith — that is, anyone confident in belief. (Do people who truly love their spouses have to defend their devotion at every turn?) It's inappropriate for anyone who no longer sneers at Freud, Darwin, and the Pill. But more in line with the hope of this book, the ghetto mentality that shackles the Divine Imagination to the mind-set of those who compile carefully worded Catholic compendiums smothers the *life-giving* faith. It wastes so much time and energy battling about split hairs — with people who purport to be on the same side! When, instead of erecting firmer battlements, we could be breaking open doorways, welcoming to more abundant life.

When we declare that Jesus "rose again in fulfillment of the scriptures," we need to be acknowledging only that the Hebrew scriptures are *one more* indication that death-and-rebirth are clearly inveterate habits much to God's liking. Again and again, they tell the same story with different characters: arrogant self-sufficiency precipitates tragic downfalls, which in turn invite Israel back to their covenant with Yahweh, which then brings victory and a new beginning. The same can be gathered from the 14 billion years evidencing God's endless dissatisfaction with status quos all over the universe and his creative ingenuity in starting over. Since the beginning, evolution reveals that same onward process in the fusion of simpler elements resulting in higher-level entities. Closer to home, it happens so frequently we no longer appreciate it as miraculous: the recurring rhythms of life renewing itself from birth to death, the seasons moving predictably but always differently from one to the next, the eternal discontent of the still-alive human mind with stagnation, constantly insisting "There's gotta be a *better* way!"

That pattern at least suggests that God would be highly unlikely to allow death to be "The End" of our lives. Invariably, God seems irreformably "into" recycling into better forms.

Ironically, satanically, it's precisely that God-given restlessness that commercials suborn in order to send us hankering for transitory pleasures that quickly turn hollow, outmoded, obsolescent. That same old "Adam and Eve Story" with different costumes and new rhythms. But no matter what our point of view on God, even indifference, and no matter how much we achieve, "our hearts are restless till they rest in Thee." It's a God-size hunger. Always has been.

Despite our parochial minds, we have more in common with other humans than our training encouraged us to appreciate. We all share the same stages inviting us to grow, from birth itself to old age and the prospect of death. Our inward parts are interchangeable. We can transplant a Jew's corneas into an Arab's eyes, replace a redneck's kidney with an African American's, transfuse a nun's blood into the veins of a streetwalker. All three great Western religions are spiritually rooted in Abraham; we're all spiritual Semites. The Global Village now reveals itself as more intricately meshed than we were able to realize before. If one nation profits inordinately, everybody else has to suffer for it. The entire human race is genetically African. And at our most radical, we are all children of the stars.

The object of all our quests is enrichment of the same humanity in the same universe.

It's more profitable to believers to look to *all* scriptures — even beyond our hallowed Judeo-Christian scriptures — not for "proofs," the smug conviction that we are right and all the rest are wrong — but for insights into who God is and what God expects of us. What's more, no matter what we were taught, God didn't have to stop revealing his truth at the death of the last disciple of Jesus. Nor does he restrict access to himself through any particular religious tradition or practice. Nor indeed even solely through avowedly religious writers and speakers. Long before there was writing or even speech, God began manifesting himself at the instant of the Big Bang.

Story and Truth

We've already seen that symbols can often convey more truth than definitions. The clear dictionary definition of "love" says less about that reality than a little girl's meticulously corn-rowed hair or a boy at the doorway with a fistful of dandelions saying, "For you, Mommy." God imagined as a great Spirit hovering over the original chaos, or thundering to Job from a whirlwind, or hanging in torment from a cross "says" more than the most brilliant theologian could capture. And far more souls are transformed by living stories than by dissected syllogisms — the way religion is *still* (against all both-lobe reason and experience) being taught by well-meaning people more interested in indoctrination than conversion.

Stories can work the same way symbols do, coming at a truth "around the corner," engaging the listener in ways carefully reasoned texts so often fail to do. The author of Genesis had no illusions that his audience believed snakes once talked to naked ladies in the park, any more than Aesop, writing about the same time, thought his listeners were simple enough to believe rabbits and turtles laid bets on a race. Jesus quite obviously made up stories like "The Good Samaritan" simply because the lawyer who provoked it would have rejected him out of hand if Jesus had said, flat out, there's no limit to "Who is my neighbor?"

For that reason, it's the height of naivete either to suspend reason entirely like fundamentalists or to allow reason to tyrannize as cynics do, when faced with what are clearly symbolic stories in scripture, like walking on water. Any attempts to explain that by postulating a sandbar or enormous lily pads or a whale suddenly thrusting itself up in the Lake of Tiberias miss the whole point of the story, just as simpleminded as sneering at the story because it's physically impossible. The point (which both extremes of literalism miss completely) is not that Jesus walked on water, but that *Peter* "walked on water." The story "says": If you forget your own shortcomings and keep focused on Jesus calling, you can do what you thought impossible. Quite likely it won't mean you can defy the laws of physics (although the God who invented them need not be shackled by them). Still, the complete coward of Holy Thursday could endure crucifixion head-down rather than deny his experience of the risen Jesus. That's a miracle.

It would be not only unfair but foolish to hold the scriptures to the same standards we now demand of the evening news. Although the New Testament did intend to testify to the historical truth, its *primary* goal was to testify to the Good News: amnesty from the fear of meaninglessness and death. Those books are meant to be more persuasive than informative.

Terry Eagleton exposes the simplemindedness of either literalist extreme: "Like trying to convince you, with fastidious attention to architectural and zoological detail, that King Kong could not possibly have scaled the Empire State Building because it would have collapsed under his weight."

Scripture is precisely the place where we need the same wonder as quantum physicists.

Our education has been shockingly unbalanced in favor of the coldly rational skills and insights that prepare us for the dog-eat-dog struggle to make a living. And that situation gets much worse year after year. Pragmatism trumps altruism at every juncture. But that simplemindedness completely dismisses one-half of the total human potential to understand, the skills that make us not only shrewd as serpents but gentle as doves. To make war, you need the cunning; to agree to and administer the peace, you need the adaptive.

If a symbolic story is to do its job, we have to momentarily short-circuit the calculating intelligence, just as we do when we ignore that people on stage are pretending that their most intimate self-revelations are not being watched and heard by a few hundred eavesdroppers out in the dark. Just as we do when we pray. The composition of place technique or *lectio divina* allows us to get into the scene and relive it in ways our two-thousand-year perspective can make even richer than the circumscribed understandings of the original listeners, and certainly better than the eyewitnesses! There is no doubt we are able, legitimately, to interpret the Christian truths in ways inaccessible to people limited to a first-century cosmology and theology. In the very same way, even a hundred years after the events, Gospel writers "inserted back into" their reportage convictions the later Christian community had discerned in the intervening time, like Thomas declaring "my Lord and my God" (John 20:28). The early Church councils did exactly the same when they tried to clarify confusions about the Trinity and the nature of Christ, based on the belief that the Holy Spirit remains "with us." Today, the better-trained "elders" in the Christian churches claim to do exactly the same: take on the viewpoint of Jesus to evaluate situations a first-century mind could simply not have imagined, like atomic war, morning-after abortion, stem-cell research. (A very real and substantial problem does arise today when more than a few in the pews are now often "better trained" than those in rectories, chanceries, and administrative offices of the Vatican.)

How do we know if later interpretations are justified? Jesus answered that, too. "You will know them by their fruits. Are grapes gathered from thorns, or figs from thistles?" (Matt. 7:16). Does the story make those who accept it more self-righteous, touchy, judgmental, exclusive, incapable of growth, resistant to joy? Or does it qualify for what St. Paul called the validating gifts of the Holy Spirit: an increase of "love, joy, peace, patience, kindness, generosity, faithfulness, gentleness, and self-control?" (Gal. 5:22–23). Simple as that.

Other Holy Scriptures

A time-worn story tells of a half-dozen blind men taken on a walk through a Calcutta park. Somehow or other, their nurse fell into a well or ran off with the gardener or got abducted by an alien spaceship. Whatever, they were abandoned, left to feel around and get themselves un-lost. Suddenly, one cried out, "I found a wall! Maybe there's a gate." Another said, "No, no, I can still feel tree stumps." A third said, "You're right. Big palm leaves up there." Still another screeched, "Agh! There's a big snake up in one of those trees." The fifth said, "Oooh! A spear! Are you a guard? Can you help us?" And the last one said, "Yech! There's a rope hanging from the wall. It's smelly, but maybe it's a bell."

As you probably figured, they'd all found an elephant. Every one of their opinions was "wrong," but not completely. Even putting all their circumscribed experiences together, it still takes an intuitive right-brain leap to synthesize them into a whole elephant rather than a quite inadequate "sum of its parts."

From the pagan primitive's obeisance to the Thunder God to the Everywhere God we now know coruscates in the furthermost galaxy and our innermost cells, we're all pawing around exactly the same "Object." In "the old days," protective churchfolk kept us from the insights of other seekers. Many of "their" sacred and secular books were locked away in chicken-wire cages even in seminary libraries, in the days when one couldn't attend Harvard without the bishop's permission, rarely given. There was a papal *Index of Forbidden Books*, and as a requirement for ordination, every seminarian had to kneel in the sanctuary and take a solemn oath against Modernism, required by Pope St. Pius X.

What were we afraid of? Contamination by corrupting ideas? A weakness in Catholic training that would leave us open to the seductions of falsehoods? Or even a fear that exposure to more reasonable ideas might lead us to find flaws in our own Church?

No need to hearken all the way back to Galileo. Pope Pius IX (1864) condemned religious freedom: "[It is an error to say that] every man is free to embrace and profess that religion which, guided by the light of reason, he shall consider true." Even Pope Leo XIII, who issued the great labor encyclicals, wrote in 1888: "It is contrary to reason that error and truth have equal rights." Others, among them even certified saints, insisted that "outside the [Roman Catholic] Church there is no salvation." For centuries that was a major motivation for missionary activity: hope of baptisms to save poor benighted souls from hell, even without willing conversion, even through inhuman tortures.

Worth recalling that at one time the official Church — and a host of other Americans, many with no formal religion at all — felt exactly the same about world communism, unshakably enough to engage us in wars in Korea and Vietnam, hideously wasteful of human lives.

Jesus was less fastidious and judgmental. He did, in fact, criticize the "little faith" of his followers, but he showed every sensitivity to the unsure: "He does not break the bruised reed nor extinguish the smoking flax" (Matt. 12:20), and he seemed more than pleased with the father who cried out, "I believe. Help my unbelief!" Moreover, in the parable of the weeds, he showed that assessment of our choices should be left to his Father — and, at that, not till the final judgment (Matt. 13:24–30).

It's wise also to keep in mind that the first pope backed down, twice, publicly, over doctrines he had previously believed non-negotiables of Christianity: circumcision (Acts 15:10) and the Jewish dietary laws (Acts 10:9–15). Wise, too, to recall that the great St. Paul was quite wrong in accepting slavery as part of the divine plan and gave substance to Augustine in negative stands on the intelligence of females, which each might well have tempered had they encountered Catherine of Siena, Teresa of Avila, Bridget of Sweden, or Dorothy Day.

Thomas Aquinas (1227–74) also wrote: "Every judgment of conscience, be it right or wrong, be it about things evil in themselves or morally indifferent, is obligatory, in such wise that he who acts against his conscience always sins." Even when the conscience is objectively wrong.

In a more jocular vein, Cardinal Newman wrote to the Duke of Norfolk (1874): "I shall drink — to the Pope, if you please, still to conscience first and to the Pope afterwards."

But easement for Catholic minds came in Vatican II (1962–65) in such statements as:

– This Vatican Council declares that the human person has a right to religious freedom. This freedom means that all men are to be immune from coercion on the part of individuals or of social groups and of any human power, in such wise that no one is to be forced to act in a manner contrary to his own beliefs.

– At the same time, the charity of Christ urges him to love and have prudence and patience in his dealings with those who are in error or in ignorance with regard to the faith.

– In the first place we must recall the people to whom the testament and the promises were given and from whom Christ was born according to the flesh [Jews]. . . . But the plan of salvation also includes those who acknowledge the Creator. In the first place amongst these there are the Mohamedans, who, professing to hold the faith of Abraham, along with us adore the one and merciful God, who on the last day will judge mankind. Nor is God far distant from those who in shadows and images seek the unknown God, for it is He who gives to all men life and breath and all things, and as Savior wills that all men be saved.

– The Catholic Church rejects nothing of what is true and holy in these religions. She has a high regard for the manner of life and conduct, the precepts and teachings, which, although differing in many ways from her own teaching, nonetheless often reflect a ray of that truth which enlightens all men.

– While rejecting atheism, root and branch, the Church sincerely professes that all men, believers and unbelievers alike, ought to work for the rightful betterment of this world in which all alike live. . . . She courteously invites atheists to examine the Gospel of Christ with an open mind.

To those non-Catholics to whom the official Church finally humbled herself, these statements quite possibly seem to carry a whiff of condescension. It could be interpreted in the same way as saying, "If you just want to get someplace, a Hyundai will do the job just fine. However, this Bugati will get you there in *style*. It's the real thing."

But for people who value evenhandedness, it's only fair to realize what a *seismic* shift Vatican II was. This is the Church, remember, that took four hundred years to yield to the truth of Galileo. The same Church which, on the Good Fridays of my youth (not that long ago) prayed against "perfidious Jews," pagans with "iniquitous hearts," infidels, and schismatics.

Finally, Pope John Paul II (1996) addressed the Pontifical Academy of Sciences under the title, *Truth Cannot Contradict Truth:* "New knowledge has led to the recognition of the theory of evolution as more than a hypothesis." Hardly openhanded endorsement, but that admission is light-years from the *Index* and the Oath Against Modernism. Granted, there seems to be in today's Church a concerted effort to "reform the reforms." But we have to trust in the Spirit that no one will succeed entirely in closing the windows, or the minds, that Pope John XXIII flung open.

Who Acknowledge the Creator

All scientific discoveries began, not in the analytical, discursive brain but with an intuitive hunch: in *wonder*. "Maybe if we fiddle with this bread mold we could find a medicine we'll call penicillin." Or "something with those stars — or that chemical change, or those silicon chips is . . . *intriguing*. I wonder. . . ." Genuine learning begins *only* in wonder, or it never begins. You can have submissive acceptance of data, like programming a computer, or indoctrinating Hitler Youth, or selling greed on TV. But you'll never find anything gripping, stirring, life-enhancing that doesn't first ignite a felt *curiosity,* an itch to probe further.

Just so, all genuine religion begins — not as it did for most of us, with indoctrination and imposed worship — but with a personally captivating experience, a "sense" of the numinous, a presence larger than the capacities of this world to produce it. Apparently the earliest humans had the awareness they inhabited a larger dimension than the constrictions of their daily lives. Powers all around them — in wind, earth, fire, water — were too intense for their containers. Or growth can begin with Peggy Lee's puzzlement: "Is that all there is?" Or distress at the inadequacy of what "everybody says" about God, with doubt, with an honest confrontation with the fact that God *doesn't* answer my prayers the way they told me God would. Or the rock-bottom human question: How could a good (or even just a basically decent) God allow innocent suffering?

From my limited standpoint, I can call out to any other believer at his or her differently privileged place around the same "Elephant," and ask, "What do He/She/They look like from where you are?" Some reports are going to jar with my experience and preferences, like Methodists' distaste for alcohol and dancing and Muslims' and early Mormons' discontent with monogamy. But leaving our religious practices and penalties aside, where can their insights *excite* new convictions about God and our religious connections, notions that (contrary to what has now become patently obvious about God) we've allowed to become stale and grace-less?

Unlike the rationalist approach we inherited from the great Greeks, Eastern minds and religions are more supple, more comfortable with openmindedness, discovery, complementarity. They are, ironically but in fact, more attuned to the more buoyant mind-set of quantum physics!

Hinduism: The earliest religion we have much knowledge about is Hinduism (before 2000 B.C.E.). In contrast to its proliferation of major and minor gods, its focal belief is the *unity* of all beings, and in the end all its other gods are simply manifestations of the One, Brahman. Just like the insights of Teilhard de Chardin, they believe every object, every person, every space is saturated with the sacred. To the dismay of our urge to schematize all realities, the Brahman is one and many, becoming and unchanging, personal and impersonal, fullness and emptiness, good and evil. The Brahman, in fact, not only defies categories but is even beyond all *predicates*, beyond even "is" and "exists."

Atman is the soul — both the world-soul (the Platonic *anima mundi*, Bergson's *élan vital*, Teilhard de Chardin's noosphere) or the individual soul-self, the animating spark of the divine Brahman. A yoga teacher once put it very movingly: "I bow to the divine in you." "Atman *is* Brahman" asserts in an equally mystifying and intriguing way: "Matter *is* energy." We can find a kinship also with that same enlivening insight in Jesus' final discourse at the last supper (John 14–17): "So they may be one, just as you and I are one. I in them and you in me, so that they may be completely one." The *essence* of Hinduism is yielding to that cohesive oneness — not to be *saved* but to be *liberated*. As St. Paul wrote, "It is no longer I who live, but it is Christ who lives in me" (Gal. 2:20).

More, Hinduism, the faith of Gandhi, is admirable in its toleration of other viewpoints on the Ultimate Reality: "The truth is one, but different sages call it by different names."

Buddhism, like Protestantism in the West, arose in reaction against Hindu excesses: exploitative castes, venal priests, rampant theologizing, mystery degraded to superstition. To counter those excesses, Gautama Siddhartha (the Buddha, the Enlightened One) evolved a system of self-discipline which had no authorities, no castes, no elaborate ritual, no speculative theology, no shackling traditions. We in the West might not be comfortable with such undefined laxity, but pondering Buddhist insights might urge us toward a better balance between clarity and intuition.

Our own sense of religion (*religare,* to connect) rests on a person-to-Person relationship with the God who not only created but sustains, with whom we are psychically engaged. Buddha neither accepted nor rejected a *personal* God outside the human dimension.

The Buddhist soul is like an onion; when you peel back the last leaf... nothing. Unsettling as that is, we can recall the views of some modern scientists who say that, when you burrow down to the inside of the most basic atomic particle, you will find non-extended Energy. St. Paul said, "so that God may be all in all" (1 Cor. 15:28).

Confucianism is not so much a "religion," a divine connection, as a moral code. Confucius wandered, trying to find ways by any means possible (street talks, entertainment, education) to inculcate virtue in ordinary people by first converting the selfishness of their rulers. Although his attention was on this-world behavior, his use of the words "the will of heaven" as the source of an *inner* moral imperative implies at least some kind of purposeful Ultimate Being.

From his study of Chinese classics, he distilled a set of doctrines called the Tao (Dah-ow), the Way to Heaven, not through codified laws but by the contemplation of *people* who were in fact humanly fulfilled. The cult of ancestors, which Roman authorities condemned as idolatry when they heard of it from the first missionaries to China, is no more idolatry than the Christian Communion of Saints. It is a belief that those who have gone before are still part of our family, and their example, like our lives of the saints, can show us the way to human fulfillment. As we have seen, in today's world, where the tabloids have made heroes an endangered species, such models are sorely needed, though they could well seem naive to our overly stimulated and distracted young.

Most readers have seen the symbol of the Confucian Tao, a circle (which is an infinite line) bisected by a single constantly wavy line, one side white (the masculine *Yang*), one black (the feminine *Yin*), yet each with a spot of the other color embedded within it. It is a perfect whole, fluctuating yet balanced. One can't say it's a white circle with a black curve, or vice versa. It is a synthesis of *Yang* — hot, dry, active, light, movement, fire, heaven, male, and *Yin* — cool, moist, receptive, dark, rest, water, earth, female. A total balance, a synthesis of rest and movement. Its flexible complementarity is the diametric opposite of pernicious Western dualism.

Judaism is, at its depth, Eastern not Western. Before the Christian interpretations that irritate my Jewish friend, before its scriptures were used like scholarly research justifying the accession of a new king, before its elucidation by Christians heavily influenced by Greek rationalism, Judaism is a much more visceral than cerebral religion. It is far more warmly personal than coldly rational. The Hebrew understanding of "know" was grounded not in sound reasoning but in the verb for sexual intercourse, by which a husband and wife "knew" one another. The basic metaphor for Jews' union with God wasn't a legal relationship (despite Deuteronomy) but the marriage covenant between Yahweh and Israel on Sinai.

"Hear, O Israel, the Lord our God, the Lord is One," is the daily Jewish prayer, wrapped in the mezuzah at the doorway of Jewish homes. Even for nonpracticing Jews, Jewish identity *is* their history with God: struggling against fertility cults, slavery, corrupt worldly kings, and always the threats of "the strangers' ways" to dilute their identity. God is holy, utterly transcendent yet present: *Emmanuel*, "God with us." He is biased toward the outcast and downtrodden. Even the verb "to be" has no meaning except "to be *with*," with God and the People.

Islam. "There is no God but Allah, and Mohammed is his prophet." Every Muslim hears that called from the minaret by the muezzin five times a day. Our obligation to God is to bear witness, keep his sovereignty always in mind. In sharp contrast to developed Western countries, a Muslim male doesn't "leave all that religion to the little woman." Rather than a catalogue of beliefs, Islam is a core conviction; the very word "Islam" means "submission, resignation," to the irresistible will of Allah. Although a great many scholarly books have been written elaborating complicated laws, Islam is far closer in spirit to the Jewish mentality than to the Greek. And like Judaism and medieval Christendom, Islam is not simply a religion but a whole *culture.*

For the Muslim, the Koran (*Qur'an*) is the book that brooks no doubt, dictated to Mohammed through the angel Gabriel. In contrast to the comradely immanence of God in both the Jewish and Christian view, Allah is utterly transcendent, like the Ultimate Deity of Eastern religions. Thus, prayer for the Muslim is a one-way conversation. Nonetheless, every chapter of the Koran begins: "in the name of Allah, the Compassionate, the Merciful. . . . " That God is merciful to those who submit to his will, manifest in "the way things are."

Muslims are exemplary in manifesting their beliefs concretely, beyond question. They pray five times each day: on rising, at noon, mid-afternoon, after sunset, and before bed. Their charity is evident: 2.5 percent — not just of that year's income, but of their total wealth — to the poor. Every year in the month of Ramadan, a good Muslim abstains from sunup to sundown from all food and drink, even in desert heat, to discipline the self and to understand the plight of the poor. Once in a lifetime, Muslims are urged to travel to Mecca to underline their common humanity, despite their social status, and their common belief, despite their nationality.

Protestantism. The two essentials of Protestant Christianity are preaching the Word of God and administration of the sacraments, which most restrict to two: Baptism and the Eucharist. They constitute a bewildering array of "Protestantisms" allowing complete freedom of belief. Luther held to the Real Presence in the

Eucharist, but he and his followers were vigorous in stripping away the "idolatrous": tabernacles, crucifixes with a body, statues of saints, stained-glass windows, and ornate ceremonies. The focus of worship was the word and the Eucharist. Those who remember the pre–Vatican II liturgy and churches lament the sense of majesty now missing in today's Roman Catholic Church. The Presbyterian churches originating with John Calvin of Geneva are governed by presbyters or elders elected from the area, and few hold for the Real Presence. It is easy to find Calvin's God too harsh. and his view of God's wishes too stifling. (Consider the Pilgrims.) Anglicans are a spectrum of beliefs and practices ranging from High Church, little different from Catholicism, to Low Church, similar to Baptists. Although they are also varied, Baptists share several common beliefs. First, they are all "evangelical," i.e., the normative Bible is stripped of most doctrines evolved after it was written. Their worship varies with the tastes of the community, from sedate Quaker prayer services to Pentecostal exuberance: speaking in tongues, jumping, shouting, dancing, remotely akin to Catholic charismatics. In recent years, their contagious enthusiasm has converted many Catholics for whom the new sedate liturgy is too staid and remote from a declaration of commitment.

At rock-bottom, perhaps the critical point of departure of all Protestant traditions is refusal to submit to the sovereignty of the pope — a doctrine that recently has come into much stronger contention even among still-practicing Catholics, particularly about the unyielding papal insistence on the immorality of artificial birth control, the Church's positions on celibacy and female priests, and its awkward handling of the problem of priestly predators. Polls show conclusively that the great majority of churchgoing Catholics have settled their souls about denying the Church's stand on birth control in practice, but that disheartening intransigence sticks in mind when other new issues arise.

We will consider the qualifications of the Roman Catholic Church later, but for the moment, keep remembering that faith is a calculated risk. On the one hand it is *not* (as high school seniors still relentlessly say they're told) a "blind leap in the dark," which is utterly stupid. Nor, on the other, is it an assent based on absolute certitude. Just as every other opinion, including choosing a spouse or a career, and even the dependable assertions of all the "hard" sciences, the best you will ever get (short of heaven) is a high degree of probability, what Thomists call "moral certitude."

To underline our common helplessness in capturing God, the great Christian theologian Thomas Aquinas himself reputedly said at his death that, before the Reality of God, all his work was "straw." Then we would be prudent to temper our hopes that we can capture the Lord of the Universe and History in a syllabus or catechism.

Which of the nearly endless points of view on "The Elephant" seem to you, personally, to be closest to "the words of eternal life"? As Wally Kuhn, a senior wise beyond his years, once said: "All the boats leak. The trick is to find the one that leaks *least*." Those of us who remain with the pope in the Barque of Peter, even the popes who seemed more like Ahab than the fumbling fisherman Jesus chose, feel we need only one hand at the tiller.

No matter what you've heard of the fate of those who "leave the Church," the decision belongs to a bipolar mind — not merely rational but intuitive. The real criterion is "The Goldilocks Test": This one is too hard. This one is too soft. This one is just right (sort of).

Whatever Is True

Until it was abrogated by Pope Paul VI (1966), the *Index* forbade Catholics to read any author whose works might offer even the slightest temptations to disbelief. The names of only some of the many authors condemned, first published in 1559, was reissued most famously in 1905 by Pope St. Pius X. This partial list might show those who believe Vatican II was too hesitant just what a quantum leap the Roman Church has made:

Machiavelli – Kepler – Hobbes – Kant – Hugo – Erasmus – Galileo – Swift – Stendahl – Zola – Copernicus – Descartes – Locke – Balzac – Gide – Luther – Pascal – Hume – Dumas (both) – Kazantzakis – Rabelais – Milton – Voltaire – Mill – Sartre – Calvin – Spinoza – Rousseau – Flaubert – Graham Greene

For some unknown reason, Karl Marx, Charles Darwin, James Joyce, and D. H. Lawrence didn't manage to qualify, but vigilant professors certainly warned of the serpents lurking within.

Now we have shed the moral corset of censorship and allowed even those who differ from us as profoundly as atheists to have their say in forming our opinions. Personally, I found my faith profoundly *strengthened* by reading unbelievers like Samuel Beckett, Jean-Paul Sartre, Albert Camus, Christopher Hitchens, and Richard Dawkins. I came away from their bleakly noble assessment of life saying, "If they're right, I'd rather be wrong."

Karl Marx may have disdained the inescapable truth of "original sin" (no matter what its roots), which inevitably collapsed or wrenched out of kilter any society that tried to embody his ideas. *But* he does have a corrective view on a monopoly capitalism, which squeezes the many to enrich the few. One ought not to play *Monopoly* with human lives. I for one forgive Copernicus, Kepler, and Galileo for being "wrong" about the heliocentric solar system. Voltaire's *Candide* is a very salutary satire on a smug religiosity that should never be covered up, and his scorn of unbridled optimism is seconded by the existentialists, a few of whom won the Nobel Prize for Literature. I don't like Kazantzakis's Jesus, but I love his Zorba.

"I disapprove of what you say, but I will defend to the death your right to say it." It's probable Voltaire didn't even say it, but the statement is no less admirable for that.

"What do He/She/They look like from where you are?" Even if you swear it's just a wall, some snake-filled trees, a sharp branch, and a smelly rope, and there's no Elephant there at all, I'm grateful for your contribution to my still-growing understanding.

Like Jesus calling Peter out onto the water, the God whose intelligence defies comprehension never ceases to call us to come further. He defies encirclement, but he invites a lifetime of leisurely exploration. The quest is programmed into the nature of the universe and the nature of our souls. Our frame of reference is truly far more immense than we ever could have imagined.

Wow.

EIGHT

The Holy Spirit

I believe in the surprises of the Holy Spirit.
— CARDINAL LEO SUENENS

A friend once asked, "Why do we hear so little about the Holy Spirit?" Do you recall anybody giving you a satisfactory insight into what supposedly happened to you at confirmation?

I suspect one very big reason for that silent avoidance is that the Holy Spirit of God is way *too* awesome, too defiant of the rational formulas so precious to formal theologians. They love to haggle over such niceties as whether God is really the same person caught in three different operational postures (Modalists), or whether the three admittedly different personalities of God are the same substance (Arians), whether the Spirit "proceeds" from both Father and Son (Romans) or just the Father (Orthodox). Some (Semi-Arians) reduce the Spirit to the status of an angel. Others (Muslims, Unitarians) negate the Trinity entirely. Although I can only imagine the ardent curiosity such heavy questions stir in the ordinary reader, I confess they bore me blithery. To challenge my indifference and pursue the inner workings of the Divine Self, read Leo XIII, *Divinum Illud Munus* (1897), John Paul II, *Dominum Vivificantem* (1986), the *Catholic Encyclopedia* or the *Catechism of the Catholic Church* on the subject. I surrender in mute acceptance.

Despite the delicacy of their reasoning, such inquiries seem to me to arise in people as dull-souled and heavy-handed as those who would try to saddle a unicorn.

However, at the other end of the spectrum between rigid rationalism and slapdash subjectivism, talk of the Holy Spirit is also what I suspect makes even the most confident believers a touch edgy with Catholic charismatics or Born-Agains who routinely ask if you've been "slain in the Spirit" yet.

I find my proposal to ignore both incisiveness and emotionalism seconded by a mind not known for either fuzzy thinking or enthusiasm, John Calvin of Geneva: "There is no worse screen to block out the Spirit than confidence in our own intelligence."

This Spirit is both too elusive and too combustive. Even John the Baptist felt inadequate: "I baptize you with water for repentance, but one who is more powerful than I is coming after me. . . . He will baptize you with the Holy Spirit and fire" (Matt. 3:11). There is much more to this Spirit than the negativity associated with sin and washing. This is the Spirit that brooded over the primeval void, who evoked the promise in emptiness, who turned chaos into cosmos. This is the Spirit who led the Israelites as a cloud by day and fire by night. "For she is a breath of the power of God, and a pure emanation of the glory of the Almighty" (Wisd. 7:25). This Spirit overshadowed Mary and quickened the Eternal Son in her womb, whose felt presence perhaps deserted the human Jesus in the Garden, who re-enlivened him in the tomb, who burst forth in a windstorm and fire on Pentecost. For Hindus and Buddhists, this is the Brahman who ignites the Atman in each of our souls. She is akin to what Carl Gustav Jung called the Anima, the salvific feminine within a male that redeems him from savagery.

Trinity

"The Holy Spirit descended upon him in bodily form like a dove. And a voice came from heaven, 'You are my Son, the Beloved; with you I am well pleased'" (Luke 3:22). There you have all three persons of the Trinity encompassed in one verse. Another tempting scriptural site is Genesis (18:2–3): "[Abraham] looked up and saw three men standing near him. When he saw them, he ran from the tent entrance to meet them and bowed down to the ground. He said, 'My lord, if I find favor with you, do not pass by your servant.'" Abraham sees three shining presences, yet he addresses "them" as "My lord."

There are many analogies that try to simplify the Trinity, all of which limp. St. Patrick supposedly used the trefoil shamrock coming from the single stem. Others find a comparison with air-candle-flame. One that we've seen is a magnet — two different poles generating a power neither has alone. Another is that the Spirit is (at least remotely) like selfless love generated between two human persons. Or the Spirit is the soul the Father and Son breathe into the Church, the still living Body of Christ. Dorothy Sayers uses the analogy of a human artist and her creation. The Father fully expresses himself, his Word, the Son, and the love which that self-expression generates is their Spirit.

No matter in what inexplicable way the three Persons work out their internal relationships, we do stand and declare week after week that "We believe in the Holy Spirit, the Lord [Yahweh], the giver of life." Perhaps this chapter can infuse more energy into those words than they've held till now.

Spirit

> The wind blows wherever it pleases. You hear its sound, but you cannot tell where it comes from or where it is going. So it is with everyone born of the Spirit.   — John 3:8

Why is it so easy to "physicalize" the Father and Son in the wise elder on the throne and the carpenter of Nazareth, but the best we can conjure for their Spirit is a dove? No fear of anthropomorphism with the "masculine" aspects of God. Is it uneasiness with the "feminine," the same uneasiness we feel with determined women like Joan of Arc, Mother Courage, and the mother of the Maccabees? Mother Teresa and Martha in "Virginia Woolf"?

It's unfortunate that the penetrating thinkers who dominate the Quest for God in formal religions are so uncharacteristically slovenly in their interchangeable use of the words "sex" and "gender." The most astute commentators do it — resulting in unnecessary pain and frustration. With the quite rare exception of hermaphrodites, "sex" is a matter of simple objective fact: male *or* female. Lift the diaper, there's your answer. It's unarguably physical: either/or. "Gender," as anyone who's studied a foreign language ought to know, is masculine/feminine. It's psychological, a judgment call: more/less. All the stereotypical qualities wrongly restricted to the male (Jung's *animus:* clarity, analysis, logic, assertiveness, "the left brain") really ought to activate in the female as well as in the male. Likewise, all the stereotypical qualities wrongly restricted to the female (Jung's *anima:* ambiguity, synthesis, intuition, inclusiveness, "the right brain") ought to activate in the male as well. Hemingway clearly asserted the "masculine" qualities, while Robert Browning seemed more in touch with his "feminine." Margaret Thatcher and Hillary Rodham Clinton possess not only the "masculine" attributes, but are also mothers. Ironically, most of the world's most famous poets, artists, and chefs have been male.

Macho men and doormat women have never realized that any virtue, without its opposite, inevitably transforms into a vice. Justice without mercy becomes vengeance. Chastity without passion becomes sterility. Females without confidence and males without kindness become caricatures. Less than whole persons. Yet *both* are "made in the image" of a triune God.

To be healthy, any soul (*psyche*) — male or female — should be "androgynous."

We have to allow the same complementarity to the sexes as we do to electrons! Even the most resistant admit that, outside time and space, God has no genitals and thus is neither male nor female. But in my insouciance, I see no reason why the gender of God must be unrelievedly "masculine," since the God who invented earaches also invented music. We need only reflect on the "feminine" sensitivity of Jesus to weakness, especially sexual weakness, though he himself had never suffered from sin. (If there was any disjunction in characterizing Jesus in our training, it was making Jesus *too* "feminine," allowing the Lamb of God to gobble up the Lion of Judah.)

From the time of the First Covenant, a harsh, daunting picture of God appealed strongly to (mostly male) thinkers and writers, both in Judaism and in Christianity: God is my "rock," my "mighty fortress." Although Greek and Latin don't ordinarily explicitly use pronouns as the subjects of verbs, at least English translations always have even Jesus using the masculine pronoun even about the Spirit: "If I go, I will send him [*eum:* masc.] to you. And when he comes, he will prove the world wrong about sin and righteousness and judgment" (John 16:7–8).

Unfortunately, despite a general acceptance of the equality of the sexes, that head-trip addiction to clean-cut dualism still waxes strong. Women who chafe against the aboriginal tyranny of the "masculine" have long been considered overly educated "cranks." The U.S. Catholic bishops' subcommittee on the "conformity" (their word) of religion texts to the universal *Catechism* expressed, in 2004, serious distress with textbooks that demonstrate "a studied avoidance of revealed proper names or personal pronouns for the Persons in the Blessed Trinity. This leads to an inaccurate understanding of the divine nature of the Persons of the Trinity as well as their unity with each other and their proper relations. Some of the texts [try] to avoid masculine titles or pronouns for the Persons of the Trinity."

Writers in Hebrew, Greek, and Latin were less fastidious about subject-pronouns than we, so it calls for abdication of intelligence to accept that pronouns for the Trinity are "revealed."

There needn't be any kind of prudish "impropriety" in conceding that God is not exclusively hard-nosed and demanding. The Confucian Tao suggests the same opening of our minds and imaginations, breaking free of the God-images and God-propositions of our training. Rudolf Otto studied the this-world power and presence of God (the Holy Spirit) as the *mysterium tremendum*, "the overwhelming mystery." But that reaction of smallness compared to the immensity of God needn't be restricted to terror. It could also validly describe the kind of fascinated helplessness — the "Oh, my God!" moments — when we encounter a star-strewn summer sky, a storm-ravaged sea, a newborn child. Not so much "fear of the Lord" as stunned awe.

Aldous Huxley tried to capture it: "The incompatibility between man's egotism and the divine purity, between man's self-aggravated separateness and the infinity of God."

The "Feminine" in God

Genesis 1:2 says: "So God created humankind [*adam*] in his image, in the image of God he created them; male and female he created them." The inspired author was moved to say God created "them," not "him," and that they were *both* created "in the image of God." Clement of Alexandria (c. 150–215 C.E.) wrote: "In his ineffable majesty, he is our Father, but in the comfort he extends to us, he has become our mother." Ease with complementarity, which Trinity requires from the very start, would accept both Father and Mother — coexistent. Even the doughty Leo XIII, in *Divinum Illud* on the Holy Spirit, seems to make an uncharacteristic and divinely inspired slip: "*She* earnestly implores Him to wash, heal, water our minds and hearts" (emphasis added). Even the most conservative clergy are comfortable calling the Church, the Body of Christ animated by God's Spirit, "she."

There is no need to wrench our imaginations and our lifetime liturgical habits to insist on equitably rotating "Our Father" with "Our Mother." That aspect is already there, in their Spirit, if only we freed ourselves from our enslaving metaphors and the constrictions of valid word usage.

Almost every religion seeks a relationship with God that is not only companionable but intimate. Hebrews described the this-world presence of Yahweh as the *shekinah* ("luminous indwelling"), the divine aura that hovered over the Ark of the Covenant. The word is feminine. *Ruah*, Hebrew for "breath of life," is feminine. In Latin, *anima*, betokens both breath and soul. To be impartial, Greek pneuma ("spirit, breath") is neuter, but psyche ("soul") is feminine.

The Holy Spirit *is* the Mama who flicks on the light, hugs us, and says, "It's okay, honey. Everything's just fine now." She is "home," a matrix of meaning to hang on to, a background perspective against which everything can be measured so that it "makes sense."

Philosopher Sam Keen describes spirit, in God and in ourselves:

> Spirit, like wind, is visible only in the movement that results from its presence. We see trees swaying, the breath moving through the cycle of inspiration and expiration, but we do not see the thing itself. Soul, like light, can be detected only by what it illuminates. We must creep up on the intangible quarry, and when we are in its vicinity we can detect its presence or absence.

You can discern the presence of the Holy Spirit by her fruits: "love, joy, peace, patience, kindness, generosity, faithfulness, gentleness, and self-control" (Gal. 5:22–23). Even in the religiously unaffiliated.

Scripture

Until 1454, the cathedral basilica of Constantinople was called *Hagia Sophia:* Church of the Holy Wisdom of God. Then it became a mosque; now it is a museum. (There is a probably unwarranted temptation to see a symbol there.)

In the Book of Wisdom, we get an insight into the Spirit's spitfire assertiveness:

> For she is a breath of the power of God,
> and a pure emanation of the glory of the Almighty;
> therefore nothing defiled gains entrance into her.
> For she is a reflection of eternal light,
> a spotless mirror of the working of God,
> and an image of his goodness.　　— Wisd. 7:25–26

And yet she is also the patient mother, waiting to serve:

> One who rises early to seek her will have no difficulty,
> for she will be found sitting at the gate.
> To fix one's thought on her is perfect understanding,
> and one who is vigilant on her account
> will soon be free from care,
> because she goes about seeking those worthy of her,
> and she graciously appears to them in their paths,
> and meets them in every thought.　　— Wisd. 6:14–16

In scripture, acts are attributed to the Spirit that are ascribable to God alone: creation — "while the spirit of God swept over the face of the waters" (Gen. 1:2) and resurrection — "If the Spirit of him who raised Jesus from the dead dwells in you, he who raised Christ from the dead will give life to your mortal bodies also *through his Spirit* that dwells in you" (Rom. 8:11). The Spirit was the agent of Christ's birth — "The Holy Spirit will come upon you, and the power of the Most High will overshadow you; therefore the child to be born of you will be holy; he will be called Son of God" (Luke 1:35). The Spirit testified to Jesus' Sonship at his baptism — "And just as he was coming up out of the water, he saw the heavens torn apart and the Spirit descending like a dove on him" (Mark 1:10); then the same Spirit "hurled" Jesus into the desert to have his Sonship tested (1:12). When he emerged from his ordeal there, he gave his inaugural address in the synagogue, the Spirit validating his ministry — "The Spirit of the Lord is upon me, because he has anointed me to bring good news to the poor" (Luke 4:18).

One of the lengthiest expositions of the Spirit's role comes in Jesus' farewell discourse at the last supper (John 16:5–16). The Spirit will be sent by the Father and the Son. Her mission will be to take the place of the Son in the role he played during his mortal life as a helper for the benefit of his disciples. The Spirit will intervene and act as a replacement for Christ, adopting the role of Advocate or Paraclete, "a public defender."

"I still have many things to say to you, but you cannot bear them now. When the Spirit of truth comes, [she] will guide you into all the truth" (12–13). That could be said of us now, even after — and in many ways despite — the training that led to our confirmation. Probably at age twelve. Few insights we would rely on dependant on the capacities of a prepubescent child. Even at that age, especially today, the one gift children have always had that might help us relate to God more richly — their capacity for wonder and enchantment — has long since been overwhelmed.

At his death: "Jesus, crying with a loud voice, said, 'Father, into your hands I commend my spirit.' Having said this, he breathed his last." But on Easter evening, he appeared to "the disciples" (Note: not just to the eleven apostles) and, "he breathed on them and said to them, 'Receive the Holy Spirit'" (John 16:22). At the very end of Matthew's Gospel, Jesus seals their mission: "Go therefore and make disciples of all nations, baptizing them in the name of the Father and of the Son and of the Holy Spirit" (Matt. 28:19). Then a month later:

> When the day of Pentecost had come, they were all together in one place. And suddenly from heaven there came a sound like the rush of a violent wind, and it filled the entire house

where they were sitting. Divided tongues, as of fire, appeared among them, and a tongue rested on each of them. All of them were filled with the Holy Spirit and began to speak in other languages, as the Spirit gave them ability.

Note again: They were "all together," not just the eleven apostles. The fiery commission descends on "all of them," not just the future pope and bishops. This is quite another "side of God" from the one revealed by Jesus in the father of the prodigal, the God who is tender with sinners and outcasts. The same God who cherishes also challenges. Occasionally, we see God as "our refuge and our strength." At other times, God is the God of Job who lays on us impossible burdens, not least of which is the call for trust, even at the moment God seems to betray it.

C. S. Lewis describes that *Mysterium Tremendum* we dare call "Father/Mother":

The great spirit you so lightly invoked, "the lord of terrible aspect," is present: not a senile benevolence that drowsily wishes you to be happy in your own way, not the cold phi-lanthropy of a conscientious magistrate, nor the care of a host who feels responsible for the comfort of his guests, but the consuming fire Himself, the Love that made the worlds, persistent as the artist's love for his work and despotic as a man's love for a dog, jealous, inexorable, exacting as love between the sexes.

"The Sin against the Holy Spirit"

Truly I tell you, people will be forgiven for their sins and whatever blasphemies they utter; but whoever blasphemes against the Holy Spirit can never have forgiveness, but is guilty of an eternal sin. (Mark 3:28–29)

This unforgivable sin is mentioned by all three Synoptics, so it's unlikely to be an insertion by an overly judgmental monk copyist. And the warning comes from the same Jesus who later enumerated a great many of the "sins and blasphemies" that, however heinous they seem, he says in that previous quotation can nevertheless be forgiven:

> Wicked designs come from the deep recesses of the heart: acts of fornication, theft, murder, adulterous conduct, greed, maliciousness, deceit, sensuality, envy, blasphemy, arrogance, an obtuse spirit. (Mark 7:21–22, NAB)

Since the first handy catechism, moralists have been ever ready with inclusive lists, enumerating the major contenders for that sin beyond forgiveness. *Despair:* As in the case of Judas, believing one's sins are beyond forgiveness, in the extreme leading to suicide — either immediate and dramatic, or gradually and corrosively with drugs or alcohol. *Presumption:* Assuming either that God forgives everybody, even those who feel no need or inclination to ask forgiveness or, like the Pharisees whom Jesus wanted to forgive, because they were smug in their certainty that their law-abiding rectitude had bought God's approval. *Envy:* Begrudging the goodness of others, sneering at their naivete, corrupting their innocence. *Obstinacy:* Clinging to pet sins, rhapsodizing their needs over others', refusing to yield center stage to Anyone but themselves. And *impenitence:* Those seemingly incapable of regret or remorse.

In the New Code of Canon Law (1983), suicide is no longer an impediment to burial in sacred ground. Before that, it was considered an amalgam of all five candidates for the "unforgivable sin," but now, allowing for the insights of modern psychology, it's obvious that individuals in full possession of their wits could kill themselves. Those same advanced psychological discoveries also offer us the unpleasant conundrum of sociopaths — those constitutionally incapable of conscience, apparently "victims" of a kind of moral autism. Are they "responsible"? If they are utterly incapable of feeling any empathy, at the very least all but the most inaccessible can understand "the rules of the game," which justifies society in punishing those who fail to live within those rules. As for their afterlife, let us be grateful such decisions are out of our hands and that such definitive judgment will wait till "the end of the age" (Matt. 13:40).

With no qualification other than common sense, I'd suggest that all those listed sins are variations of a single mind-set: knowingly not wanting to be forgiven, not feeling the need for it.

Most scripture quotations in these pages are from the New Revised Standard Version (NRSV), which translates the final sin in Jesus' list as "folly," which the New American Bible (NAB) translates as "an obtuse spirit." The Greek is *aphrosune:* senselessness, thoughtlessness, recklessness — egotism. The Latin is *stultitia,* which means, bluntly, "stupidity."

I wonder if there might be justification to revert back to Hannah Arendt's insight into the ordinary men and women who numbed themselves to the utmost in human degradation in the Nazi camps, who threw responsibility for indefensible evil away from themselves with "I was only following orders." I wonder if the unforgivable sin might be culpable persistence in simply being *dumb.* As Oedipus — and Judas — proved, "dumb" has nothing to do with inadequate education or deficient IQ. The unforgivable sin is impenetrable self-enclosure.

The task of the converted Christian is to rescue anyone we can from "dumb."

Confirmation

What gifts were supposed to accrue in our souls at confirmation and almost certainly did not — simply because we weren't mature enough to have the remotest appreciation of what they were? Almost all kids are confirmed before puberty. We wouldn't allow marriage or a vow of celibacy for anyone so inexperienced, yet we do urge them to (supposedly) "accept" a lifelong commitment to Christianity at that unformed and uninformed age. But one cannot (repeat: *cannot*) appraise Christianity in any genuine way until long after the painful assimilation of all adolescence entails — not to mention surmounting the more seductive temptations and the more rigorous tests of our faith that can intrude upon most of us only *after* a sheltered schooling.

The official Church states unequivocally in Canon 97, no. 2: "With the completion of the seventh year, however, a minor is presumed to have the use of reason." Anyone naive enough to actually "presume" that has never had a teenage child or taught high-school sophomores.

A prepubescent child is not yet even on the outskirts of the quest for meaning — which is what genuine spirituality means. No one should dare believe even older teenagers have the wherewithal for that Quest. It's begun, surely, but it will take a long time and a great deal of seasoning for it to be achievable. Although they're beginning to feel the *need* for a myth, they don't yet have the skills even to reason clearly and objectively about anything, especially about anything that intrudes on their freedom.

And Christianity reaches far beyond the desire to be "just" a good, moral person. (If that doesn't come *first*, Christianity doesn't stand a chance.) They can't grasp Christianity, which can be reduced to only two words: "forgiveness" and "resurrection." How can a child apprehend and value those realities when, in the modern ethos, (1) guilt trips are to be shunned like the plague and (2) one's own death is so remote as to be still unreal. (Attend the funeral of a teenage suicide or accident victim and *feel* the incomprehension.)

Confirmation is a lost opportunity for a meaningful rite of passage. In primitive societies, a girl was isolated at her first menstruation, the shock and uncertainty soothed by the women.

Understanding the seismic shift from child to adult is more dramatically disruptive, less easily ignored for girls, since nature lets them know, willy nilly, they are no longer children. For girls, physical maturity means suffering; for boys, it's an unexplainable pleasure, and as we see in our society, that pleasure can become completely dissociated from any sense of responsibility.

In some primitive societies, boys at the time of puberty were stranded in the wilderness. Then at night, men came yowling at the boys, covered in garish paint, brandishing knives and slashing themselves. Then they circumcised the boys. With a stone knife. The men did to the boys what nature had done to their sisters: making them aware this new power in them was not something to be toyed with. After those nights, no boy or girl was unaware that the whole world had changed.

In our society, that important moment is lost, partly due to our being more "civilized," but also being less in touch with the human truths about embodied spirits, because of the very fact of our learning and sophistication.

Baptism, as Dr. Monika Hellwig explained, is an Easter event: an experience of resurrection; confirmation is a Pentecost event: an experience of missioning. Aquinas wrote that what differentiates confirmation from baptism is that, while baptism empowers one to receive the other sacraments, confirmation provides a power to profess one's faith in words. However, according to some dissenting (and authoritative) modern theologians, such empowerment "would lead in the twentieth century, to such aberrant interpretations of confirmation as a sacrament of Catholic action or as a sacrament for the ordination of the laity." But that is the Gospel: the Spirit came on "all of them" (Acts 2:1–4), and that mission is corroborated by Vatican II: "Bound more intimately to the Church by the sacrament of confirmation, they are endowed by the Holy Spirit with special strength. Hence they are more strictly obliged to spread and defend the faith both by word and by deed as true witnesses of Christ."

Confirmation ought to reflect a *personal* conversion, and yet those who discern the meaning and determine the qualifications for it are people who haven't dealt with adolescents since they shed their own adolescence. Like adult converts, those to be confirmed need a growing awareness that the Gospel is *true* and its truth *internalized*. They need a felt sense of belonging. And a sense that this act is not just a commission but a felt commitment.

Is it heresy to decry and deny Canon 97, no. 2?

Unless you yourself really understood your own confirmation at the time — with all the adult responsibilities it entails, plus all the insights into being Christian now available to us that weren't even thought of then, this book has found its purpose.

The gifts that were given us then — almost beyond argument too soon — were the enlivening power of the windstorm and the emboldening power of the firestorm. What we were incapable of grasping was what it meant to be adult Christians, rather than Christian children. Why? Because we were nowhere near to *being* adults. The enormous gifts that slipped through our unready hands were discernment and empowerment from the Spirit who breathes both light and heat.

Lord of Light: Discernment

The kingdom of heaven is like treasure hidden in a field, which someone found and hid; then in his joy he goes and sells all that he has and buys that field. (Matt. 13:44)

Metaphors are more confusing than meaningful unless we decompact them.

Okay, you're boppin' along in your field and your toe hits something. You peer down and, lo, it seems to be a box. You paw around it and, whaddya know, it *is* a box. You snap off the lock with a rock, creak open the lid, and Wow! It's *filled* with diamonds, rubies, pearls, and gold! And it's all *yours!* I don't know about you, but if that happened to me I know I'd shout — helplessly — "Holy [*beep*]!" Resurrecting Wow.

Which means that, if you ever actually *understood* the Good News — that our sins are forgiven and that we need never fear death — you simply *must* have shouted, "Holy [*beep*]!" And if you haven't, if being Christian hasn't made you feel the same liberating exhilaration a paroled convict feels, then quite likely you've never even *heard* the Good News yet. Even if you felt all your Christian learning was behind you.

Now, does it take more than one set of fingers to count how many Christians you know who have been *that* helplessly exuberant about being Christian? Are many of them clambering up onto the rooftops to shout that Good News? If all that ol' Catholic brainwashing had been even the least bit successful, I'd imagine our rooftops would be a lot more crowded.

The Lord, the Giver of Life: Enspiriting

A.A. has a good many bumper-sticker truths, which remain truths despite their brevity and frequency. One is "Let go and let God." That sounds appealingly consoling. But it's a lot more burdensome than it first appears. It's the same incautious concession we've mouthed so often without assessing the cost: "Thy will be done." As C. S. Lewis said, when we invite God in, we invite not only the attentive Good Shepherd but the fire and whirlwind of Pentecost, who will not content herself with merely sprucing up the decor of our tiny temples, or even just clear out the unpleasant debris. She wants to fire us up and send us out on the road! Isn't that what she did with Jesus? Difficult to ponder a crucifix and still content oneself with being "reserved."

When God gives gifts, like sacraments, they almost always come with an unsettling challenge attached. Not just empowerment but an insistence on putting it to good use. In a sense, Pentecost was analogous to parents multiplying themselves by pushing their children out of the security of the Upper Room toward confident independence.

If we actually *grasp* that, it really ought to be more daunting than most practicing believers might have understood. All the people to whom God offered his friendship in scripture were smart enough to be aware of its cost. Not a single one of them — from Genesis to Revelation — was an emissary any of us would have picked for the tasks, and most of them realized that and did their utmost to elude it.

God is notoriously on the prowl for dullards to inspire. Consider "the history of salvation" and its utterly unlikely heroes:

At the very start, the Eden Experiment was a failure. So of course you cut your losses and start over from scratch. No proper manager would start over with the *same* pair who botched the whole initial enterprise. Except God. Later you decide to found a dynasty you'll eventually call Israel, and you're searching for the grandparents of a tribe more numerous than the stars. Would any reasonable person seek out Abraham and Sarah, in their nineties and barren as a pair of bricks? In fact, yes. God did. Further on, when their descendants have managed to get themselves enslaved in Egypt, and you plan on rescuing them, you look for a hero along the lines that Cecil B. De Mille did when he chose chesty Charlton Heston. No, the omniscient God sends his Spirit after someone more like Elmer Fudd, who stammers, spends a whole page trying to weasel out of the assignment, and agrees only if he can give all the good speeches to his brother, Aaron. Do we begin to see a pattern here?

The Philistines have this humongous fighter named Goliath who needs disposal, so you send your agent, Samuel, to Jesse, who has eight sons. You interview the first seven, who are the size of Schwarzenegger with muscles like snake-pits. "Any others?" Well, there's David, the spindly kid with a slingshot who tends the sheep. He'd be lost inside a suit of armor. That's our man! Later, when the problem is the Midianites, the Spirit seeks out Gideon, whose own mother would admit he's the biggest coward in the village. And God tells him to send away any recruits who aren't also cowards. Go figure. Then the problem is Nineveh, so God approaches Jonah, whose main talent is minding his own business. Shrewdly, Jonah sees the utter futility of God's request and hightails it in the opposite direction on a ship bound for Spain. But when the crew pitches Jonah overboard to placate a storm, God has this huge fish waiting to gulp him down and fin his way back toward that Nineveh.

The prophets' polite protestations are also on scriptural record. Besides the reluctant Moses, Isaiah countered his invitation with: "Woe is me! I am lost, for I am a man of unclean lips, and I live among a people of unclean lips; yet my eyes have seen the King, the Lord of hosts!" (6:3). And Jeremiah, who also has a stammer: "Ah, Lord God! Truly I do not know how to speak, for I am only a boy." But the Lord said to me, "'Do *not* say, 'I am only a boy'; for you shall go to all to whom I send you, and you shall speak whatever I command you!" (1:6–7).

Which brings us to the final restructuring of the mission. If you wanted to find the mother of the Messiah, surely you'd send the Spirit to search out Rome or Athens or Alexandria. Would you even dream of going to a no-name village in a no-name province to a hillbilly girl, and ask her *permission*? Any need for further evidence that "God's ways are not our ways"? There's more! You're going to organize the definitive campaign. We'll call it Christianity. So to mastermind it, you pick Judas, who has connections in high places and an eye for a shekel. No. He picks the big-hearted, thick-headed one, who understands what you say just enough to get it totally backward, who at least has the good sense to say from the outset, "Go away from me, Lord, for I am a sinful man!" (Luke 5:8). The very one who said, "Even though I must *die* with you, I will not deny you" (Mark 14:31) — then denied you three times in one night, with fierce oaths, not to a soldier with a sword at his throat, but to a *waitress!* Right!

The dullest soul can see a preferential option here that opens an insight into God we may never have noticed. We are called by a God who found no difficulty bringing a universe out of nothing, who patiently fine-tuned his creation for billions of years, who gleefully invented the hairy-nosed wombat, the giraffe, and sex. He/She/They purposefully gave a cerebral cortex and freedom to an inadequately evolved tribe of apes, suffered the deviance of their Chosen People for centuries, managed to evolve from a ragtag clutch of cowards a community that has mushroomed into a world of cathedrals, hospitals, soup kitchens, universities, its members two billion strong around the world, of whom thousands are still martyred every year for their faith. When He/She/They became a human being, Jesus found no problem working miracles with materials as unpromising as mud and spittle.

Saying "Oh, I'm nobody" is as foolhardy as holding up a nine-iron in a lightning storm when that Holy Spirit is hovering about.

Again, I'd dare to distinguish between "soul" and "spirit." The difference, I think, is between the candle and the candle aflame. "Soul" is a potential; "grace" is the aliveness of God, the Holy Spirit, who ignites the soul — so that, if we are invigorated by the divine energy, we ought to be living lives recognizably more spirited than most other people. St. Irenaeus said, "The glory of God [what Hebrews name *shekinah*] is humanity, fully alive." The enspirited human isn't just "animated" but "*magn*animous." The "Wow!" in our lives should be readily discernible.

When she was considering Catholicism, Claire Booth Luce used to look at Catholics and say, "You say you have the truth. Well, the truth should set you free, give you joy. Can I *see* your freedom? Can I *feel* your joy?"

Nifty questions.

NINE

The Least Leaky Boat

This is the big fact about Christian ethics: the discovery of the new balance. Paganism had been like a pillar of marble, upright because proportioned with symmetry. Christianity was like a huge and ragged and romantic rock, which, though it sways on its pedestal at the slightest touch, yet, because its exaggerated excrescences exactly balance each other, is enthroned a thousand years. . . . It is only a matter of an inch, but an inch is everything when you are balancing.

— GILBERT KEITH CHESTERTON

Actual classroom interchange:

Sharp Senior: You think there's a lotta [*beep!*] in the Roman Catholic Church?

Canny Teacher: Of course! And I know a *lot* more about the [*beep!*] than you do!

SS: Then why don't you leave? You're a hypocrite.

CT: That's moronic.

SS: You callin' me a moron?

CT: Why not? You just called me a hypocrite. Look. I'm not calling you a moron. It's your *idea* that's moronic. I see a lot of flaws in the way our government embodies the ideal of American democracy. But not enough to make me pack my bags and head for Fiji.

Ideals are like the North Star — a guide, not a destination. Not only is an imperfect Church better than nothing, it is — undeniable fact — the very best you can ever get! As the wise Wally Kuhn said, "All the boats leak. The trick is to find the one that leaks least."

One might criticize what follows (as one reader did) as "suggesting a predilection against belonging, rather than an assumption that one would want to." The motivation for the chapter — and in fact this whole book — is directly contrary to that. The criticism is justified in that the book "assumes" that the appeal of membership in the Roman Catholic Church is not as reliably compelling as it once was, as many (unjustifiably, I believe) do indeed still "assume." It tries to look at the facts as they might appear to a lifelong Catholic with one foot out the door, or at least those bred to expect much better of the Church than the image painted of her in the omnipresent media and in their own experience of it in the necessarily imperfect "real world." Thus, whatever is written comes from a writer who has offered this imperfect Church sixty years of poverty, chastity, and obedience. And is still here.

No one honest can deny that the greatest obstacle to the Church is the Church. *Any* church is a reality — an ideal *embodied* by irksomely mistake-prone human beings. As long as it's lodged on this planet, it *must* be imperfect, defective, open to growth and improvement. To claim perfection is blasphemous. Just consider the very first embodiment in the Gospels and Acts, and realize that's exactly as God *intended* it to be. It's a this-world *institution*, organized and conducted and explained, from the very beginning, by humans — and by far the majority of them bookish human males overly fond of dominance.

Even people who resolutely fail religion courses can still rattle off the really baffling mistakes: the misplaced ambition of the very first apostles (which continues), the literally bloody battles over doctrine in the early centuries, the departure of the whole Eastern half in the eleventh century over doctrines few on either side could explain today (or care about), Galileo and the Inquisition, scandalous crusades, enslavement of the Americas, the Protestant Reformation, Bloody Mary of England, the struggle against modern ideas, the birth control issue (which seems to trouble only purists now), the recent abhorrent discovery of sexually predatory priests. Even the best informed of us can probably enumerate more of the faults in the Church than its overwhelming achievements. More college history papers will be written this year by young Catholics about debauched Renaissance popes than about the Church's role in spreading literacy.

What Got Lost

What got lost? To be honest: faith in "The Faith." I'll try to defend that.

Admittedly, "back then," Catholicism seeped into the fibers of people without our even realizing — as it did, I suspect, with Jews, though not necessarily with Protestants. The difference was the intensity of the encompassing beliefs and the ardor of our parents. The church or synagogue was not just a place but a whole culture, a myth system whose symbols were the very sinews of everyone's everyday lives. We were, up to the 1950s, far more "ghettoized" — and living in a surrounding national culture far more stable than our own today. Everybody in the parish pretty much knew everybody else — and their needs. We met more often, not only at Mass but at missions, novenas, the Catholic Youth Organization, bazaars, sodalities, the Knights of Columbus, not only to share a common project but a common concern for one another. Not just a congregation, as quite often today, but a genuine community. And we shared a forest of, to us, quite meaningful symbols embodying our common life-view: rosaries, medals, solemn high Masses, majestic organs rather than twangy guitars, Saturday confessions, benedictions, clerical and religious garb. We sang the same old treacly hymns all the time, but we bellowed them with conviction. It was, to be sure, a unity far more of the heart than of the mind. Like the Marines.

Then, after World War II, we became educated, better-off, and more mobile, and therefore "accepted," assimilated. But you can't be absorbed without being diluted. That's what so many older Catholics simply fail to comprehend. Our young can rightly say, "You were *never* my age."

The cliche people sometimes use, especially about no-longer practicing Catholics like James Joyce and Tom Cruise, is: "You can take the boy out of the church, but you can't take the Church out of the boy." That's only partly true, depending on the intensity of the earlier indoctrination and the psychological (soul) depth of "the boy." Any surface absorption of Catholicism will disappear faster than a dirty windshield in even a passing rain shower.

I got a call once from a young man I'd taught in his senior year of high school, asking me to "do" his wedding. I asked if they were both practicing Catholics, since the only reason a priest can validate a marriage, even civilly, is that he's a recognized representative of the Church. "Well, uh, no. She's Jewish, and we agreed to raise the children Jewish. Oh, not for religious reasons. No, no. Just ethnic reasons." Hm. I asked if he himself practiced, even sometimes. "Not really." Did he pray at all? "Not really." But why have a priest at his wedding? (Foolish question. I knew the answer: his parents.) "Well, I'm still Catholic." I said, trying for an even tone, "To be honest, you're no more still a Catholic than I'm still a Boy Scout." So I said no.

The core question — which probably even that young man couldn't answer — is whether he ever really *was* a genuine Catholic. Did he ever, at any point in those long years of formation at home and in schools or even at confirmation — did he ever truly, personally, as a knowledgeable adult *choose* Catholicism as *his* myth system? Or did it just "attach itself" to him? Was it so external to his soul that, when he'd lost it, he failed even to notice it was gone? Till his wedding.

He couldn't honestly leave the Church, because he'd never really been there in the first place. He had never, ever, considered Christianity and said, "Holy [*beep*]! Wow!"

People say they've "left the Church" when they stop going to Mass. The real reason we *feel the need* to attend Mass is an act of gratitude to the One who invited us into . . . everything. It's also a way to remind ourselves we weren't born to be nobodies; we were born to make a difference; we're Peers of the Realm: *noblesse oblige.* We have a context that eradicates the uniquely human fear of sin and death. Even without fame, we're "gonna live forever!" And when we're feeling relatively lost and alone, all those other people remind us that we're really not.

Until the fallen-away have felt that need, that God-sized empty soul-place, until like the prodigal they can say, "How many of my father's hired hands have bread enough and to spare, but here I am dying of hunger! (Luke 15:17)," unless they feel a need for all that "bread" means, it's highly unlikely they're ever going to "come home." Oh, they'll stop by for their weddings, for their children's baptisms, for their parents' funerals. Like Don Vito Corleone.

Again, "back then," despite the welter of customs and catechisms, very few Catholics "reasoned their way" to the Church. But we did personally *accept* it; we made a *gut* act of faith in the whole overarching matrix of meaning — just as nonrationally as we accepted our birth family. Even when those in charge have been remiss, or deadly dumb, or even shameless, we stuck it out. And the very adhesion-no-matter-what is precisely what gives coherence to any family. Maybe even *despite* all the enforced religion classes, the Roman Catholic Church has been "home." Holy *Mother* Church. Only in our later years could we see her flaws, but they were tolerable because of who she has been and who she always will be for us.

An unusually bright high school senior posed the problem for me perfectly: "I treat God the way I treat my parents' *other* friends." He was polite and gracious to them (when unavoidable); he visited them without too much protest; but once he was free to start his own tribe, they would almost surely never share the same space together — except perhaps for baptisms, weddings, and funerals.

Until the bishops and catechetical publishers make personal conviction (faith) their goal rather than encyclopedic indoctrination, the People of God will suffer for their myopia.

The young have to feel the need for a boat before they go in Quest of the least leaky one.

Why Stay?

If we concede the existence of a God who gave us the inestimable gift of existence — and all that's precious that came along with it (no matter the drawbacks) — such a generosity demands overt gratitude. If, say, a zillionaire gave you a million bucks, no strings, and you didn't seek that guy out and say, again and again, "Thank you!" you'd be a pretty ungrateful swine. So if this God invited you to the party *and* promised to forgive you no matter what, *and* guaranteed you'll survive death, that treasure would demand a public declaration. No one — even the nonreligious — can deny that the moments of birth, marriage, and death demand celebration, placement within an infinite matrix. A civil office issuing a birth certificate, or a justice of the peace, or dumping the corpse into a hole simply will not suffice. Those moments are simply too important. Well, what about the moment of realizing that I myself didn't do anything to merit an invitation to be here at all? I didn't exist; how could I have deserved anything? And uncountable people didn't wake up this morning, but I did! Wow! And, again, *wow!*

Chesterton wrote: "When we were children we were grateful to those who filled our stockings at Christmas time. Why are we not grateful to God for filling our stockings with legs?"

And if one accepts Jesus as the embodiment of God who said, "Do *this* in remembrance of me" (Luke 22:19), then the only question left is which Christian myth system lays the most persuasive claim to embody all those truths (albeit imperfectly)?

It's highly unlikely that, even after Pentecost, a single one of the first disciples could explain much of the Nicene Creed. But if they returned, which of the innumerable attempts at fulfilling the task they (admittedly confusedly) set out to accomplish would they find most "comfortable"? This isn't rocket science; it's faith. It's the Goldilocks Method.

The world itself after two thousand years would astonish them. None of the four great Christian communions — Roman, Orthodox, Protestant, Anglican — would, on the surface, seem anything like the small clusters of Christians in the first century who met each Sunday to hear the word of God and share his Supper. The simplest catechism would present dumbfounding theological and moral problems, which have evolved naturally out of twenty centuries' study of the original Gospel message and arising to cope with realities that weren't realities for them. And they would be hard put, as many of us are, to see a common ground in the liturgical opulence of the Orthodox liturgy or the grandeur of St. Peter's, on the one hand, and the bleak simplicity of a Quaker worship meeting or the vocal and physical enthusiasm of a fundamentalist Baptist prayer meeting on the other. But, given a little time to assimilate, which might feel closest to "right" to them?

To depend exclusively on painstaking logic or on the rush of intuition leaves us half-witted. We *understand* only with the whole "self," the soul, which fuses the inconclusive conclusions from both ways of knowing into at least a tentative answer, a commitment, an act of faith. Faith is a calculated risk based at best on a high degree of probability. We commit ourselves "with no rea-sonable doubt." We need to be *triple-minded,* like the Trinity in whose image we're made: coming to conclusions with the left- and right-brains merged in the soul, the whole self, who says, "Yes."

But a few norms present themselves to help with a decision.

One, Holy, Catholic, and Apostolic

There is no lack of sources like the *Catechism* to provide evi-dence that Jesus *expected* his Church to have those distinguishing marks, and that the tradition of all the Christian churches has *wanted* to embody those qualities. But the question those sources seem to ignore resolutely is whether the Church I'm in has those marks — right now.

Imperfectly One

At the last supper, Jesus prayed, "that they may be one, as we are one" (John 17:11). No human grouping can have literally the flaw-less unity of the Son and Father. Accept that, or go crazy. Nor — if you consider the disciples Jesus personally chose and their lives together after the resurrection — can you hold the slightest hope or desire for *uniformity.* Many otherwise intelligent Catho-lics over the centuries have had that misplaced expectation and demand, to our common peril and shame (e.g., the Inquisition).

First, if you're looking not for rigid uniformity but at least some measure of consistency in religious doctrine and practice, it's reassuring to have a single hand on the ship's tiller. One can with good conscience differ with the pope or the Vatican on this or that doctrine, as long as you accept what seem the nonnegotiables: the divinity of Jesus, the transcendence of reality, the call to ser-vice, and the worship-meal at which Jesus is more truly present than anywhere else in the universe. The disciples who came back would expect at least that.

Second, it is beyond dispute that the Roman Catholic Church is the original. It didn't break away from the Eastern Orthodox in 1054, nor from Martin Luther in 1517, nor from Henry VIII in 1531. It's quite possible you could find that some other Christian denomination fulfills Jesus' hopes more completely than the Roman Church, but determining that superiority honestly would take more study than merely, "Mass is boring," or "That priest was unkind." Nor could anyone honestly disallow the Church for shallow reasons like "all those rules." In the first place, what *specific* rules — besides birth control, which for most is a dead issue? More importantly, nearly all "those rules" are admonitions about simply acting like a decent human being. The Ten Commandments are embodied in just about every set of ethics that includes a Deity. And almost all objections to "the Church" are actually disagreements with "the Vatican" and not to "the Catholic People of God."

What can be said on behalf of that Body?

The Roman Church at least seems the original from which the others branched. Whether scrupulous historians can find incontestable proof of "legal" transmission of power from each single pope to the next is hardly important to someone content with "a high degree of probability." Reforming the original, though daunting, seems more promising than breaking away and starting over. As we've seen, God did do that in the time of Noah, yet things seem to have settled pretty quickly back to clumsiness as usual.

Part of the difficulty arises from a kind of "creeping infallibility," the sense in some Catholics that every statement from the pope — or anyone in Rome, for that matter — has the same unarguable binding force on a Catholic's conscience as the belief that Jesus is the embodiment of God. But that is manifestly untrue. To say that a Vatican declaration about the sanctity — or even existence — of St. Christopher is as important as a Vatican declaration that nothing justifies torture is silly. Catholic doctrine is not an unbending monolith but rather a whole spectrum of doctrines ranging from the scarcely important (the shapes and colors of vest-ments) through the serious (the manner of the Real Presence in the Eucharist) to the essential (the incarnation and resurrection).

The best directors refuse to impoverish the combined effort by making it depend solely on their own personal experience and competence. The director may have the last word, but he or she doesn't have the last idea. The enthusiasm of the liberal needs the caution of the conservative; the solid traditionalist needs the adaptable progressive. God knows the Roman Church has both.

The Roman Church is the oldest living institution in human history. For over two thousand years, it has defied probability and even the second law of thermodynamics that says everything is decaying. Despite all the internal corruption, schisms, confusions, refusals to adapt, centuries of cozying with corrupt governments, and popes who insisted visitors kiss their feet! Despite every exter-nal attempt to eradicate her: the arena and catacombs, barbarian invasions, the Enlightenment, the French Revolution, Hitler's oath that, after the war he'd "crush the Catholic Church like a toad," twenty centuries of hideous martyrdoms. Against all conceivable odds, Something more than dumb luck keeps it going.

Imperfectly Holy

The Church has too often allowed its concern for the world's welfare to yield to a desire for the world's power. She has been called, even by Fathers of the Church, the *casta meretrix*, "the chaste whore." It calls to mind the woman "known as a sinner in the town" who wept on Jesus' feet and dried them with her hair. He told his host, "Her many sins are forgiven — because of her great love" (Luke 7:47). Unlike too many pious churchfolk, the real Jesus seems to have considered kindness more noteworthy than sins.

Paradox is embedded in the fibers of all reality. We're mistaken if we define "holiness" as we would define God's transcendent goodness. To a Jew, holiness meant "wholeness," like the whole-ness of a sphere, no matter its size, having a grasp of who you are, what's truly important, where your life is headed. "Having it all together." But as we've seen so often, another inescapable constant in our reality is that there will always be room to evolve and grow. Even in the Body of Christ.

Another fallacy is Pelagianism, a heresy whose proponents insist we have to *earn* our holiness by avoiding sin and doing good deeds. Such a doctrine is evolved by people who simply can't comprehend (or even permit) unconditional love — no strings, no qualifying tests. The love a mother has for her child, even when he or she is rightfully on death row. We couldn't possibly have merited God's love before we existed; therefore, inescapably, we were loved into existence. How can we work to merit something we *already have?* But wasn't that what "they" told us?

Christ offers himself to us. When we accept his kindness, his advent *makes* us holy. For that reason, although Eucharis-tic Prayer II, in the final petition before the Great Amen, reads: "Have mercy on us all; make us worthy to share eternal life with Mary, the virgin Mother of God . . . ," that sparks a question in me: "Isn't that what Jesus already *did* for us?" Why does that liturgical segment constrain us to ask for something our faith tells us we already have?

Imperfectly Catholic

"Catholic" means the *opposite* of "exclusive," and the languages, tempos, and solemnity or enthusiasm of Catholic worship around the world is evidence of its openness. Critics could rightly assert that squabbles over the precise theological meaning and content of the Eucharist pose an unnecessary barrier to communion across Christian denominations. Again it is wise to test any Church action or attitude against the clear intentions of its Founder. In Jesus' parable of the weeds (Matt. 13:24–30), the wise farmer let both grow side by side until the harvest, lest his farmhands pull up good grain by mistake.

In dealing with the upstart Christian sect, the Pharisee Gamaliel gave his fellow Jewish elders advice the Church has herself too often ignored in the years since then:

> Keep away from these men and let them alone; because if this plan or this undertaking is of human origin, it will fail; but if it is of God, you will not be able to overthrow them — in that case you may even be found fighting against God! (Acts 5:38–39)

And in 1622, Pope Gregory XV wrote:

> Do not bring any pressure to bear on the peoples to change their manners, customs and uses, unless they are evidently immoral. What could be more absurd than to transplant France, Spain, Italy, or some other European country to China? Do not introduce all that to them, but only the faith, which does not despise or destroy the manners and customs of any people.

Unfortunately, he was one of very few popes to feel that way.

Imperfectly Apostolic

There are really three meanings to "apostolic." The one the official Church uses most often is "an unbroken linkage of popes back to Peter." A second is "a Church consistent with the ideals, if not the actual practices, of the churches of the apostles." The third is the meaning most modern readers grasp: "reaching out to others."

If you are intellectually able to leap some gaps in the papal succession — and sort through the snarls of assertions when more than one (sometimes four!) claimed the office at the same time — you could probably construct a (sort of) satisfactory chain. But if your faith in the Roman Church hinges on that, you would do well to seek support for your belief from other sources!

In the second sense, would someone from the earliest churches who came back today say, "Yes, that's (more or less) what we intended." Remember, however, that Peter, the very first pope, did in fact change his mind about two doctrines he had firmly believed had been *essentials* of Christianity: circumcision and dietary laws (Acts 15). The pope himself forgot that Jesus had said, "Do you not see that whatever goes into a person from outside cannot defile?" (Mark 7:18).

In the third sense, the "solitary Christian" is a contradiction. Jesus said, "As the Father has sent me, so I send you" (John 20:21). The visible Catholic Church is evidently apostolic, reaching out in every direction, high and low, transglobally. But in that sense, so are most other religions. But if we can say that the apostolic mission of Christ is incumbent on all Catholics, no matter their ordination or lack of it, what does it mean concretely, week-by-week?

When the rich man asked Jesus what he could do to live a fuller life (Mark 10:17–39) and assured Jesus he had kept the commandments from his early life, "Jesus, looking at him, loved him" (21). That was enough. But when the man asked for more, Jesus offered him a vocation as one of those who left everything. When the man felt unable to do that, there's no evidence Jesus held him in less regard. However, "Christian" hardly means just being a decent human being. Every good atheist wants that. Nor, I suggest, does it mean merely accepting the nonnegotiables of Christianity: the incarnation, the resurrection, them-first mastering me-first, the worshiping community. It also entails being apostolic. That needn't involve pulpits or lecterns or soap boxes. But it does mean spreading the Good News: amnesty from the fear of sin and death. We are committed (if we really believe) to *challenge* doom and gloom. Being an apostle needn't be any more intrusive than rising above our reserve to say, "I don't mean to intrude, but you seem kind of down. If there's anything I can do, you have only to ask."

The Gut Conviction

To assert that the Roman Catholic Church is the unique and only conduit to God's grace is the height of arrogance, since it pretends to set limits on the very God whose grace we value. Such claims are as embarrassing as forcing God to reconfigure the solar system and restructure His/Her/Their plan for the development of reality because human minds twenty-five hundred years ago had made the only possible educated guesses about them. God has been self-revealing for at least 14 billion years and dispensing grace to our ancestors for almost a half million years before we have even any evidence about their responses to it. Surely God has found ways to dispense genuine (not ersatz or diluted or sort-of) spiritual aliveness since before there were any churches. Anyone who accepts the Hebrew scriptures is already forced to admit that. For centuries they believed they were God's chosen people, and what parent could say that a Father can have only *one?* We who find Christianity the most congenial point of view on the divine believe we have (another) privileged inroad to the Almighty. Some of us — for a variety of reasons, not all of them left-brain rational — have settled on the Roman Catholic version. Why?

A critical issue (for me) is the Real Presence of Christ in the Eucharist. Apparently both Martin Luther and Henry VIII still clung to that, despite their other differences with Rome and despite rejection by many of their followers over the centuries. I simply *believe* it, based on the same kind of evidence on which I ground my remaining a Jesuit for sixty years, on what Cardinal Newman called "informal inference," a convergence of so many *felt* experiences that they defy logical explanation. But how does the Almighty, Everlasting, and Omnipresent Son of God manage to smallen himself into a bit of bread and wine? I haven't the slightest idea. But I accept it in the same way I accept that he diminished himself into a baby in a manger and that, long before that, he brought Everything out of Nothing. The great fiction writer Flannery O'Connor speaks for me on transubstantiation: "Well, if it's a symbol, to hell with it."

As Thomas More says in Robert Bolt's *A Man for All Seasons:* "What matters is not that it's true, but that I *believe* it; or no, not that I believe it, but that *I* believe it."

Probably the most honest reason I'm still a Catholic is the same as the reason I'm still Irish, white, male, and American — none of which I originally chose, any more than I originally chose my baptism or my early Catholic schooling. I'm also fairly certain I didn't choose to be Catholic freely even at my confirmation; I was a child of twelve or so whose advice I would hardly credit today; that was yet another "arranged marriage." But I did obliquely ratify the choice my parents made when I applied to the seminary. Only gradually, though, did my religion — my person-to-Person connection to God — reach down its own roots into the depths of my soul. It's become a friendship, and no matter how unforgivably my Friend seems to have betrayed my trust, like Job, I will not give up on him — because I have the gut conviction he will never give up on me. Without that two-way connection, I doubt I'd be able to go on.

All the Magic's Gone

Can anyone honest deny that Mass is deadly dull — *unless* you already have tried-and-true faith before you arrive?

This objection is usually raised by older Catholics — although, in a very real sense, it is also behind *all* the objections of younger Catholics who say that Mass is boring or that "nothing happens." Even when older Catholics make this claim, they don't mean "magic" in the sense of hocus-pocus. Rather they mean a sense of the mysterious, the transcendent, the majestic — the very Fifth Dimension of our lives which we gather to celebrate. It's nearly ludicrous to use the word "celebration" for an event if most of the participants sit quietly and for the most part listen, and then, when they are allowed to speak or sing, do so with all the celebratory gusto of a congregation of pious sheep awaiting execution.

How to capture the soaring majesty and transcendent mystery of the Orthodox liturgy — without its length and tedium, and without its quite un-Jesus gold and jewels? How to capture the congregational enthusiasm of fundamentalist Protestants (who seem to have no problem making converts) — without its far too simple theology and without the emptiness at its center, the sacramental absence of the Guest of Honor?

What Eldridge Cleaver said remains true: "If you're not part of the solution, *you're* part of the problem." And as the pagan Confucius says, "If I am not truly present at the sacrifice, there is no sacrifice." If you yourself come to worship as a witness and not a participant, if you sit there, politely, just waiting to get "zapped" with "eternal life," that's like expecting to find overpowering love on the first date. If you're fortified in skepticism, uptight, hating the greeting of peace, convinced everybody else is there just to show off, then a celebrant with all the talents and skills of Leonard Bernstein and Robin Williams — along with the full-throttle Mormon Tabernacle Choir and a bevy of Vegas showgirls — couldn't make you say, "Wow!"

I don't believe the Lord who forgave Peter's denials, who loved the rich man even though he couldn't give up everything, who drew people to him only when they were ready, would be at all upset if you "shopped around" for a parish with a pastoral team who resonate to your ideas about the Gospel, with a congregation you could be tempted to care about more than for fellow passengers on a bus, and for a liturgical style and music (or lack of it) which is the least inadequate for your unique personal susceptibilities. The same is true, when you feel the need of it, in choosing a priest to whom to confess. Choose someone you are rather sure will greet you as a fellow sinner, who will be happier to have you home than to probe for your reasons for leaving.

The Latin root of the word "religion" is *re-ligare*, "to bind fast." Therefore, anyone's religion is a person-to-Person connection. Whereas "morality" describes the "horizontal," this-worldly, immanent relationship each of us has with one another and the environment (regardless of the God question), "religion" adds another "vertical," otherworldly, transcendent dimension to our lives. (The directional words are in quotes because our world is not literally flat, nor is God somehow located overhead. But it clarifies the distinctions.)

The Spirit can flame out everywhere we turn. But we have to remind ourselves that, after all's said and done, the magic in the ruby slippers is Dorothy.

Forgiveness of Sins

Forgiveness liberates the soul. It removes fear.
That is why it is such a powerful weapon.
— NELSON MANDELA

Previously I adverted enough to my discomfort with "baptism for the forgiveness of sins," because the God it implies conflicts so grievously with the God embodied in Jesus. However, I find no reluctance in gratefully accepting Reconciliation for the forgiveness of sins, for those of us who have definitely passed "the age of reason" and have treated the gift of life shabbily.

Those Were the Days

Therefore you also must be ready, for the Son of Man is coming at an unexpected hour!   — Matt. 14:33–34

I don't like thinking of God lurking, like a time-study man or "a thief in the night." Nobody likes a sneak. Except for Inspector Clouseau and Kato, good friends don't "jump" one another. That's the Gospel read by bookkeepers or writers scaring children, not people who've gone *mano a mano* with God. No question God doesn't play fair. But I can't accept a God who's sneaky. How can God *not* catch us off guard? "If I ascend to heaven, you are there; if I make my bed in Sheol, you are there" (Ps. 139:8). He knows when we stand and when we sit. He knows full well when it's really inopportune to swoop in — like Hamlet, just waiting to dispatch Claudius when his stepfather's deep in sin. Pondering the father of the prodigal doesn't leave open the idea of God "pouncing."

Jesus wasn't a bean-counter. He never once made a sinner crawl or demanded an accounting of sins by species and number or demanded restitution to "balance the books." Which makes me believe (no doubt courting an *auto da fe*) that the Pharisees whom he excoriated would understand today's canonical laws, catechisms, and exhortations to perfect doctrine and practice better than his own apostles would have.

Nonetheless, that unsettling Gospel passage has a point. Not that God's a sneak, but that *we* get so embroiled in everyday pressures we forget what's truly important: having full ownership of a soul ready for God, always trying to do better (without getting paranoid or scrupulous about it). Unless God's "in our face" once in a while, like an intrusive mother or a door-to-door evangelist, we can slack off. Snuggling into "the good life" becomes more important than keeping in mind what life is for. Death's the villain of our story, but since God sketched out the parameters, Death must have a critical role to play in what we deem important.

One sweetly sadistic old retreat giver in our novitiate told a story of "a yoong lad pairked at the foot of a hill who foinally persuaded a poor gairl to surrender her hawly purity to his insayshable *loost!* But at the top of that hill, a trook slipped its clootch and harrtled into that boy's cair and killed that gairl *instantly!* An' he has to spind his loif knowing his loost sent that gairl to hell. For all *eternity!*" Very effective motivation. Even if vehicular lust eluded us in a seminary.

If the Master decided to swoop on one of us today, I doubt he'd find any of us wallowing in sin. Not people who read and write books like this. A better question is whether the Master would find each of us *awake,* fully *alive?* Would he find a servant whose presence to other servants would be profoundly missed?

Or would he find someone who had drudged through the days, treading water, coping, getting by?

The one thing that would cause me eternal grief is to meet God, not with soiled hands, but *empty* hands. To have nothing better to show for having lived but a paid-off insurance policy. If my faults and negligences aren't important enough even to give them any attention, then it follows ineluctably that *I'm* not important. Too many people think they're nobodies. But that's a self-fulfilling prophecy. If you think that, you'll *be* a nobody — no great obstacle to those around you, but no significant gift either. No matter what any of us thinks of our shortcomings, God thought enough of each of us to call us as his sons and daughters. Maybe what we ought to be cautious about is remembering we're Peers of Christ's Realm. *Noblesse oblige.*

Forgotten Motivations

Gone are the long Saturday lines outside the confessionals, adults still nervously confessing in exactly the same ways they did for First Communion. Gone is the Divine Moneylender of our youth, when everything not compulsory was forbidden (and vice versa). Gone is the rabbit warren of guilt trips.

For that, we can say thanks. But it's a mixed blessing. Because without guilt, what you get is Auschwitz, date rapes, pushers, saturation bombing, toxic waste dumps, soft porn, drive-by shooters, world economic collapse, terrorism. We're all Little League narcissists by contrast, but if we collude by our easeful indifference to that kind of world emerging, we need legitimate guilt more than we might like to admit. When fear fell into abeyance, continuing to deepen our friendship with God became much more difficult. Now it takes far more authentic faith than it used to, because there are no longer horned devils lurking around every corner ready to swoop.

Extinction of Hell

Most Catholics seem to have chucked the whole idea of hell, which looks at first to be no serious loss. After all, where in hell do they mine all that coal? Those fires have been roaring for a long, long time. But something serious, and life-giving, died with it.

If anyone has heard from the pulpit an explanation of "hell" to replace that once sovereign and indomitable motive, one worthy of someone who has also learned physics, anthropology, cosmology, and psychology, I'd be happy to hear about it.

A New Image of God

Surely without liturgists and catechists realizing, their welcome departure from the fearsome God pointed us all toward opposite but no less tragic results: the terrifying God becomes the nearly irrelevant God. Surely, the father of the Gospel story forgave even before the prodigal left the farm. But the forgiveness couldn't activate until the son came home and asked for it. If you don't think you need it, even God can't make liberation work.

If anyone has heard from the pulpit an explanation of a God who is neither a despot nor a dupe but both — balancing one another, I'd be happy to hear about it.

The Economic Metaphor

In the old days, when we sinned, we went into "debt," and, sooner or later, we had to humble ourselves, confess our sins, and beg for a "Get Out of Jail Free" card. That, of course, was blasphemous, but highly effective and thus commonplace. Sin isn't a debt to a Banker but an insult to a Friend and Benefactor. Bankers don't "forgive" debts (not until they by-God get paid back — with interest); only parents and friends do — or genuine Christians. But if we have no day-by-day, adult, personal relationship with God, a sense of that Personal insult is not likely. We fall back on the debt metaphor, and all our debts are, truly, inconsiderable. Therefore, no need to give them much thought, right?

If anyone has heard from the pulpit an explanation of what sin does to a friendship between an all-loving Creator and well-meaning fumblers (like the first pope), which deals with God friend-to-Friend rather than borrower-to-Accountant, I'd be glad to hear about it.

Mortal/Venial

Hand in hand with that debt mentality came the ludicrous dualism of mortal/venial. Surely we can understand our relationship with God by analogy to any human relationship, like marriage, in which there are no either/or offenses but rather a spectrum of insults from the trivial *through* the more serious to a terminal state where the relationship is dead. My spouse is an ardent Republican and I'm a half-hearted Democrat; irritating perhaps, but surely trivial. I flirt a bit too much at parties, not enough to break up the relationship, but not just trivial. I have sex twice with a friend; very serious now, but again not necessarily mortally final for two spouses who really love one another. I tomcat indiscriminately, not caring about my spouse at all; then the relationship is dead — at least from my side, *even though* my spouse (and God) continue loving me, as helplessly as a mother loves her son or daughter who's a hopeless addict.

If anyone has heard from the pulpit an explanation of our relationship with God that hinges consistently on references to "The Song of Songs," I'd be happy to hear about it.

But in throwing out the inadequate motives, we also pitch out an undeniable truth: you can't mock the natures of things (which embody the will of God, guides to their legitimate uses) and get away with it for long. Of course true serious sin doesn't deliver one to feral demons, but less-than-human acts do something real and damaging to one's soul, one's self. No need of hell for drunkards; they've ingested a punishment that perfectly fits

the crime. But mean-spirited swine also inflict a less obvious punishment on themselves: their punishment is to *be* swine — and
everybody knows that except themselves. And accepting "Who's-
not-human, right?" pettinesses can't help but make one petty. Like
static on a rather good radio program. That backfire is what Don
Richard Riso calls "the law of psychic retribution." Because of
the objective way the human psyche is configured, we bring upon
ourselves a kind of punishment for bad moral choices. Carson
McCullers said the heart of an inadequate person becomes "hard
and pitted, like the seed of a peach."

What's more, whether we have a relationship with God (religion) or not, we do have an undeniable web of relationships with
everyone else on the planet and with the planet itself (morality).
The psychological malaise of guilt is like the hunger in our bellies, a natural warning that things are out of kilter and need setting
right.

"Sin" is one of the most basic terms in religious vocabulary, as
common as "grace" and "God," because sin really means being
out of a relationship with the human web and with God, "out
of sync." Beyond human dignity, the Church not only preaches
penitence but promises categorical forgiveness and a healing of
that double disconnectedness.

There is unarguably a dark side to human nature, a penchant
for screwing up. That's true of no other species we know. No rock
or rutabaga or Rottweiler can violate its programmed nature. Aberration is a *constitutive* element of the human condition. Thus,
there must be some virtue in imperfection, since God made us
imperfect, and God must have known what He/She/They were
doing. Perhaps God made us that way so we could grow, evolve
ever so slowly into the kind of person Jesus was. Like any psychotherapy (soul-healing), the sacrament of reconciliation is — at the
very least — an invitation on a strictly *human*, self-interested
level, to be truly honest with ourselves about the ways in which
we have betrayed our potential selves, and those who have been

generous with us, and the whole web of humanity. Beyond that, more profoundly, it's a way of apologizing to God for abusing the gifts of life and freedom.

Humanizing

Grace builds on nature and does not destroy it.
— Thomas Aquinas

As we saw, the Greek word for sin is *hamartia,* "missing the mark." Not just making an error in judgment in a particular case, but missing the whole point of human life; not just violating a law but being completely disoriented in the Quest for a true self, a myth.

Leaving religion — the God-connection — aside a moment, that sense of guilt (when the cause is undeniably valid) is a very healthy human *feeling* within the mistreated soul that tells us we're really not okay, urging us to make things right again. And it's a feeling, *not* a reasoned decision. The decision comes only *after* we've acknowledged the validity of the feeling and conclude the bad habits have to change. The healthy human soul turns guilt into responsibility, first by acknowledging it, then admitting it openly, and then doing something to change. A.A. is resolutely nonreligious but it does realize those radical and consistent choices are essential for escaping a cramped, incomplete, wow-less life.

Simplification

To be honest, most of us find our "consciences" to be crammed, airless attics filled with contradictory strictures accumulated since our earliest days. "No, no, don't put that in your mouth. . . . Don't you see when you hurt her, she cries just like you?" They're taped indiscriminately and with the intensity of a two-foot person listening to a six-foot person. They can never be erased. (But they can be critiqued. I was twenty-six before I dared to go to bed without pajamas! My mother was still inside my skull.) We heard — and never stop hearing — do's and don'ts from the pope, the president, the boss, the spouse, the kids, in constant conflict. The sole purpose of ads in the inescapable media is to make us unhappy, discontent with who we are.

We can lessen the clutter by taking time to consider and choose what *we* honestly accept.

Sinners don't think too much of themselves; they think too little of themselves. Healthy self-esteem would never demean the self to cheat on a quiz you'll forget in less than a week. No one with a sense of self-worth would stoop to the quick lie, the easy lay, mopping only where the boss can see, parking in the handicapped spaces, spitting gum in the drinking fountain — not without soon seeing it as a cheapening of the self and making amends by sloughing off the bad habits. But such faults are so trivial we find them dismissible rather than even embarrassing.

How different our lives might be if, once in a while, perhaps once a month, we set aside a date on our calendars to be honest with ourselves. If we took time to find the tiddly ways in which we devalue ourselves, enough tiny strings to bind down even a giant like Gulliver. Time to treat our souls as prudently as we monitor our muscles and teeth?

Perspective

Any atheist, even any child, can commit moral evil, a violation of this-world relationships. Many who find religion wanting complain about "all those rules," when in fact, any decent atheist would observe most of them — or not deserve the term "decent."

However, we're so smothered by evil today we no longer even notice it, unless it's extraordinarily blatant: 9/11, Abu Ghraib, the Asian tsunami, the Haiti earthquake, the BP oil spill. We're scarcely aware of graffiti, sirens, smog, the absurd "reality" shows. Difficult to stimulate concern for the 12 million African AIDS children, or do-nothing legislators, or even two wars on the other side of the globe. So much of the moral evil just "crept up on us" when we weren't looking, as taken for granted as three meals a day. We yawn and accept TV brainwashing to lifetime infantile greed and the insatiable discontent it breeds in all of us. Without even knowing, our young — the future — ingest the realization that no one has sex in the media unless they're *un*-married, anyone in business has to develop highly flexible morals or get stomped, anybody who doesn't feel out the competition's weaknesses and grind them, is a damn fool. They believe almost unanimously and almost incurably that morality changes from age to age and culture to culture. And in our honest moments, we have to confess we ourselves aren't entirely unaffected.

Is it possible that our adult radius of felt moral awareness and responsibility doesn't go beyond the concern and self-absorbed motivation of children: fear, the lowest of motives, and hope of personal gain, just a step above it — sheerly utilitarian and self-serving? When we argue about taxes, immigration, welfare, are our reasoned consciences still pretty much circumscribed to spouses, families, jobs, and (perhaps) neighborhoods — little broader than our children's?

Freedom

Moral evil is a sin against *oneself,* in which we curtail our own freedom and gradually weigh ourselves down with countless tiny anchors of habit. It changes our characters — and by that very fact affects the people who care for us. Every moral evil is a failure to become what we might have been, and gradually it corrodes our ability to be that fullest self. Our self-absorption becomes almost literal: we devour ourselves till there's only a personality left.

Most of the limitations on our freedom are *self-imposed:* enslavement to others' judgments, gigantification of our short-comings, and at the root: fear. If we could just lay hold of our inner selves — beyond the power of others to warp that self-possession — we might find "the serenity to accept the things that can't be changed, the courage to change the things that can be changed, and the wisdom to know the difference."

Soul-awareness

Even on a strictly this-world level, starving the soul is self-impoverishing, because the soul *is* the self: who-I-am. No one sees *me*, only my body. They can make educated guesses from what I say and do about what kind of self I am, but they don't see that true self, who (I trust) will survive death. The guards in Nazi camps had bodies and brains, but the reason we can call them "bestial" is that they lost their souls. When I honestly fall in love, it's not the yearnings of my flesh or the calculations of the brain that say, "Yep! This is the one!" It's my soul. When I stand in awe of a snow-capped peak or Michelangelo's *David* or a baby's fist around my pinkie, it's not my body or mind that says, "Gasp!" It's my soul. My intellect is intrigued; my soul is stirred. It's where all that's nebulous in me resides: honor, awe, loyalty, remorse, patriotism, faith, hope, and love. Oh, the soul is there, all right. But it won't stay an ignited spirit without attention.

A requisite for that encounter with one's soul is honesty. On the one hand, we must shuck off all the "if only's" and get on with enlivening the gifts and limitations we have. "If only I hadn't. . . . " You did. Accept that, dump it, and get on with life. In the long run, conjuring ways to deny the truth is more painful than a single act of facing it down and apologizing. On the other hand, we have to face squarely the ways in which we're not living up to our human potential, either by degrading our humanity or by failing to challenge it. One can do that alone, but we do have a tendency to kid ourselves. Thus, it makes simple good sense to find someone we believe wise who will pull us up short not only when we are too easy on ourselves but when we are too judgmental. We weren't talking sacramental confession yet, just common sense.

Divinizing: The Sacrament of Forgiveness

Again, any atheist, even any child, can commit moral evil, a violation of this-world relationships. "Sin" adds another, other-world dimension to the same act. It disrupts an ongoing relationship with the transcendent Creator who allowed us to live. Unease about wilful violations of either web at least ought not to be questions of authority or obedience, law and sanctions, going against what "the Church or society tells us," but about personally *felt* respect and love. But we have to be wary of enslavement to our metaphors, to the explanations of sin that were enough to satisfy unsophisticated children. We are no longer naughty little boys and girls, much less the sluggard slaves of the Gospels, but adult children forgetful of our need to be grateful to our Father — for even considering allowing us to be.

It should seem unavoidable (even to you right now) that you *have* made "the fundamental option," like the rich young man in the Gospel. Freud said that every individual or institution or nation makes (or slides into) either one of two radical life-views: Eros or Thanatos. Eros is the life wish; it craves challenge, growth, resurrection into a better way of living. It's what impels us to sacrifice ourselves for others. Thanatos is the death wish; it craves security, a return to the womb, an untroubled status quo. Today, many aspects of being Catholic at least seem to be shackling, smothering, stultifying. For very many, even sex is not Eros but a form of anesthesia. But Eros was what impelled you to turn the pages of this, or any, book.

Whenever a penitent has finished confessing, I always say, "Well, you're a good person, aren't you?" Hardly ever in fifty years has anyone, old or young, said gratefully and gracefully, "Yes. I believe I am. Thank you." Invariably, they smile shyly and say, "Well, I'd like to be" or "I wish I were" or "You don't really know me." That's a greater indication of how they honestly view the sacrament of forgiveness than any other, and it's an invariant and sure-fire indication of their Christian conditioning about what this sacrament is for. They seem never to have been told that bad people don't come to confession. Only good people do.

Therefore, if you'll allow a clumsy metaphor into such a high-toned subject, when you seek out periodic Reconciliation, it's not as if you're taking a pitiful wreck into a collision shop. It's like a regular thoughtful check-up to fine-tune a quite trustworthy vehicle.

More important is seeing that the fundamental option deadliest to good is not evil. The most lethal, and pervasive, threat to our connection to God is bland indifference and the smug complacency of the Pharisee. As God says in Revelation: "I could wish you were cold or hot. So then, because you are lukewarm, and neither cold nor hot, I will vomit you out of My mouth" (3:15–16).

Sean Fabin, S.M., says: "The third chapter of Genesis tells us nothing about what happened at the beginning of time, but it is a story to explain what is happening *all* of the time." It's a skeletal sketch which every sin since then has duplicated: ingratitude, self-absorption, the arrogance that believes we can get along without God.

But more than that, way *beyond* sin. We have a chance to see and accept that we sell ourselves short: "Nobody can do anything about anything." Think Walesa, Mandela, Teresa, Schweitzer, Hammerskjöld, Winfrey, Bono. Think Jesus. As Terry Eagleton boldly points out: "The morality Jesus preaches is reckless, extravagant, improvident, over-the-top, a scandal to actuaries and a stumbling block to real estate agents." For all of us, confession can ask: "Am I being pinch-penny with who I am able to be?"

The Moral Practice of Jesus

Jesus never waxed wroth over a sexual sinner. In fact, sexual sins didn't seem high on his priority list. Surely not as high as they have been in the eyes of the official Church, owing to the inter-vention of Plato, St. Augustine, and others. Incandescent minds, but they were not Jesus.

Nor was Jesus irate at Judas's impending treachery; in fact he washed his feet (John 13:12), and in the moment before his arrest said, *"Friend,* do what you are here to do" (Matt. 26:50). He didn't revile Peter for cowardice, merely asked — three times — "Peter, do you love me?" (John 21:15–17). Jesus didn't consider wealth a sin; he loved the rich young man, even unable to sell all; Lazarus and his family seemed comfortable; a penniless Samaritan was no help for the victim in the ditch, and if Joseph of Arimathea hadn't been wealthy, Jesus would have gone unburied. He seemed none too cautious for the niceties of Sabbath observance (Mark 2:27) nor about enjoying food and wine; in fact, his enemies accused him of being "a glutton and a drunkard" (Luke 7:34). Even "heretics" had gentler treatment from Jesus than they could expect from the later traditional Church; according to the parable of the weeds (Matt. 13:24–30), they should be left till the harvest.

In fact, the only sinners who upset Jesus, strongly, were the clergy and Temple minions. He reacted fiercely to the hypocrisy and grandstanding of the Pharisees, resorting to some rather insulting (not to mention imprudent) terms: "Frauds, blind fools, hypocrites, blind guides, vipers' nests" (Matt. 23). And one can almost hear Jesus grind his teeth confronting the thickheaded materialism of his own twelve seminarians. What's common to these offenses is their consistent refusal to see anything wrong with their suppositions, no sense of a need for repentance, since the rectitude of their convictions was unquestionable to them.

Perhaps the root sin is the narcissism that refuses to admit one did wrong and the inertia that finds it too much effort, too embarrassing to go back to the first wrong turn and start over.

But Jesus also offered forgiveness aplenty. When Peter asked how many times we must forgive, Jesus told him "seventy times seven times," and if God expects as much of us, we can expect at least as much of God. Though sinless himself, Jesus had a remarkable empathy for weakness. Quoting Isaiah, he said, "He will not break a bruised reed or quench a smoldering wick" (Matt. 12:20). God himself can't penetrate souls impregnable even to the Spirit's movement suggesting something is amiss and needs forgiving.

Unconditional love and forgiveness of debts is difficult for us to comprehend. Even catechesis (still) pictures a God so ego-bruised by Adam and Eve there could be no love from God till every last shekel of ransom was paid in the blood of Jesus. Which is, however well-intentioned, blasphemous. Our sins do nothing to God; their effects are in *us,* even though we refuse to see them as self-servingly as Dorian Gray.

The key, as so many Gospel stories show, is opening the eyes, submitting to the cure of our blindness. Jesus didn't come to hawk guilt; he came to offer freedom. As he said in his inauguration "platform" in the Nazareth synagogue, he was sent to declare the Year of God (Luke 4:16–19): unconditional amnesty for those willing to avail themselves of it. As the four episodes here prove conclusively, in no single case was there need to crawl, to vacuum the soul of every peccadillo, to submit to a retaliatory penance — much less "the temporal punishment due to sin" even *after* an all-merciful God has forgiven. Unconditional amnesty. The *only* requisite — in the moral practice of Jesus — was admitting one's need of it.

The Woman Known as a Sinner (Luke 7:36–50)

Simon the Pharisee had invited Jesus to dinner, though Simon forgot or forbore the courtesy of offering his guest a greeting kiss and water to wash his feet. As they dined, a woman known in the town to be a sinner entered and stood behind Jesus' couch, weeping. She wiped the tears from Jesus' feet with her hair, kissing them and anointing them with oil. Simon fumed; if Jesus were a prophet, he'd know what kind of woman this was. *His* rectitude was at stake, not her shame. But Jesus pointed to the woman: she, a known sinner, had done for him everything the upright Pharisee had failed to do. "Therefore, I tell you, her sins, which were many, have been forgiven; hence she has shown great love." The woman *said* nothing. No careful catalogue of sins; no pleading. She merely came to Jesus and humbled herself. And all her unspoken sins were forgiven. Jesus said nothing about restitution or atonement. "Your sins are forgiven." Period.

The Adulterous Woman (John 8:1–11)

As Jesus was teaching in the Temple, Pharisees brought a woman who had been caught in adultery. (Nothing said of her consort.) According to Mosaic law, she should be stoned; what did he say? Jesus merely bent and began tracing in the dirt. When they persisted, he said, "Let anyone among you who is without sin be the first to throw a stone at her." And he bent back to his puzzling tracery. Gradually, the accusers drifted away, leaving only Jesus and the woman. He finally looked up and said, "Has no one condemned you?" She replied, "No one, sir." And Jesus said, "Neither do I condemn you."

Again, no questions like the ones priests my age were taught to ask routinely: "What caused this? Are there problems in your marriage? Are there any other sins? And the sins of your past life?" No homilies, and surely no anger — only quiet acceptance and the admonition to avoid doing it again. Jesus offered *understanding*.

The Samaritan Woman (John 4:4–40)

On a journey through Samaria, Jesus stopped at a well and sent his disciples to the village for provisions. A Samaritan woman came to draw water and expressed surprise that he, a Jew, would ask water of a Samaritan.

There was an easy, teasing banter between them, playing on the idea of the water in her well and water that gave eternal life. When Jesus asked her to call her husband, she answered forthrightly,

"I have no husband." And he replied (surely with a grin), "You have had five husbands, and the one you have now is not your husband. What you have said is true!" But Jesus didn't pursue her multiple sexual unions. Instead, he spoke about something more important, a time when, soon, "true worshipers will worship the Father in Spirit and truth." At that the woman ran to gather the villagers. And when the disciples returned and begged Jesus to eat, he replied, "I have food to eat that you do not know about." Any confessor who has set a penitent free knows that repletion.

The Prodigal Father (Luke 15:11–32)

The clearest insight into Jesus' (and God's — and therefore our) treatment of sinners is this story. The only character in both parts is the father, the one the storyteller wanted his audience to identify with. Note the details.

When the younger son demanded "his share" of the estate, the father didn't say, "What? It's *my* estate that I've worked a lifetime for!" Instead, he gave it, as blithely as God gives us life, without strings, unconditionally, to do with what we choose, even against the divine will.

When the boy had frittered it away, reduced to feeding swine, he *saw* his mistake and headed for home, making up a memorized confession. But the father saw him a long way off "and was filled with compassion." Which implies the father was out there every day, hoping. And the father ran to the boy, not the other way around, threw his arms around him and kissed him. *Before* he apologized. Then the boy got out only the first sentence of his speech before his father hushed him: "Quickly, bring out a robe — the best one — and put it on him; put a ring on his finger and sandals on his feet. And get the fatted calf and kill it, and let us eat and celebrate; for this son of mine was dead and is alive again; he was lost and is found!"

The father didn't say, "I want an account of every shekel before you get back into this house!" Nothing of the shame the boy had caused him, because at the moment the boy's shame was more important than his own. Not a penance but a *party!* Because the lost sheep had found his way home. The whole Gospel: forgiveness and resurrection.

But there was another son, just as blind and perhaps farther from "home" than the profligate had ever been. He found the cause of the merriment and slumped into a sulk. But notice again the father came out *to* the son because the son refused to come in and celebrate his brother's rebirth. The older boy could think only of what *he* had done for his father, forgetting that, without his father, he would never have existed. Like so many, he had tried to merit the love his father had already felt for him nine months before he had ever seen the boy's face. *Hamartia.* His self-absorption had blinded him to the whole point.

A Matter of Emphasis

When I was fifteen, our retreat-giver read us St. Teresa's vision of her place in hell. I'm pretty sure I confessed sins I didn't even know how to perform, just to be sure. The Jesus I now know from the Gospels would, I think, have squirmed just as uncomfortably as Stephen Daedalus did through the epic retreat disquisition on hell in *Portrait of the Artist as a Young Man,* which owed more to Dante and Fr. Arnall's fevered imagination than to anything Jesus said or did. There is a kind of sadomasochistic delight too many churchfolk (on both sides of the confessional screen) have taken in the idea of a vengeful God alien to Jesus.

On the other hand, Jesus does talk of punishment. The God he pictured and embodied is not a Cosmic Patsy who forgives anything, even when we have no inclination to apologize. The key to Jesus' moral practice — in every case, without exception — does involve the humility to admit one has wandered and to come home.

But of the nearly four thousand verses in the Gospels, Jesus speaks of hell in Mark only once, in Luke three times, in Matthew six times, in John not at all. He speaks of judgment in Mark only once, in Luke twice, in Matthew and John six times each. In his lengthiest consideration of judgment (Matt. 25:31–46), the crucial question pivots on none of the sins Jesus mentioned earlier ("fornication, theft, murder, adultery," etc.) but on the sole issue of one's sensitivity or obtuseness to the suffering of Jesus in the hungry, the thirsty, the imprisoned.

Contrast the relative rareness of Jesus speaking about hell or judgment with the profusion of times in the Gospels when he both spoke and acted as one come to heal and to forgive and you come away with a picture of Christian moral practice far different from what many Christians have been led to expect.

There is no doubt we sin. There is no doubt we too often blithely slither off the hook and become amnesiac about our faults. But there is also no doubt that, according to Jesus, being forgiven ought to be a great deal easier than we fear.

When we approach the sacrament of reconciliation, we take one liberating step away from self-deception. We become not just the observers of our weakness but its accusers. We move beyond admission of guilt to a desire to be *whole* again.

Therefore, when pondering what confession really ought to be, one should be aware — but also be wary — of official pronouncements by speculative theologians on the subject.

For instance the *Catechism* (1453) says: "By itself however, imperfect contrition cannot obtain the forgiveness of grave sins, but it disposes one to obtain forgiveness in the sacrament of Penance." That is surely true. Without the gift of Christ's intercession on Calvary, no conceivable act of submission on our part could "atone" for an insult against an infinite God who gave us everything. However, in contrast to that *Catechism* entry, Jesus seemed quite content with the father who said, "I believe! Help my unbelief!" (Mark 9:24). Even when the one in need could not be 100 percent changed, there was no difficulty. Zaccheus (Luke 19) gave back "only" half of what he had exploited; the rich young man couldn't bring himself to sell all he had and come out on the road, but nonetheless "Jesus, looking at him, loved him" (Mark 10:21); the Samaritan woman at the well heard nothing from Jesus about leaving the man she was living with — even though he was her sixth. Jesus says to her merely: "What you have said is true" (John 4:18), and then goes on to talk about more important things than sin: living life more abundantly.

The *Catechism* (1459) also reads: "Raised up from sin, the sinner must still recover his full spiritual health by doing something more to make amends for the sin: he must 'make satisfaction for' or 'expiate' his sins. This satisfaction is also called 'penance.'" The closest I find to a penance in the moral practice of Jesus is his telling the adulterous woman (John 8:11), "Go your way, and from now on do not sin again." The father of the prodigal didn't give his son a penance but a party. Amnesty means unconditional forgiveness. You have only to come home and ask.

Perhaps an old Jewish story sums up that way of forgiveness, which finds little understanding or sympathy with minds conditioned to win, even at poker or Monopoly and most definitely in the game of bruisable egos. A rabbi's son has run away, and the rabbi calls to him, "Come back, my son!" And the boy shouts, "I *can't* come back!" And his father cries, "Then just come back halfway." And the boy replies, "I *can't* come back halfway." And the father says, "Then come back as far as you can. I'll come the rest of the way."

The *Catechism* dodges defining "the temporal punishment due to sin," which the *Catholic Encyclopedia* does define as "punishment due to sin, *even after the sin itself has been pardoned by God*" (emphasis added), which the Council of Trent declared was inflicted "in this world or in purgatory." The *Catechism* does face the issue when speaking of indulgences (1498); it declares that "through indulgences [easements resulting from specified prayers, pilgrimages, acts of mercy] the faithful can obtain the remission of temporal punishment resulting from sin for themselves and also for the souls in Purgatory." Again, we encounter a view of God which requires his giving forgiveness only conditionally, not unequivocally. Anthropomorphism at its absolute worst. It also assumes a God who continues to punish souls in purgatory until someone "bribes" them out or "ransoms" them. I needn't belabor my belief that this flies directly in the face of the God who stayed unflinchingly with the wayward Israel, whose Son forgave without qualifications, and who requires us to forgive those who trespass against us 490 times, *each*.

Use the sacrament of forgiveness not just to find where you've failed to value your relationship with God, but also where you failed to appreciate how good you are.

Anthony de Mello had a prayer where God intrudes on the one praying and says, "I'm so grateful for you." Obviously the one praying is befuddled and asks how that could be. And God replies, "Surely, you would be grateful beyond words to anyone who did for you even a small part of what you did for me. Do you think I have less of a heart than you?"

Wouldn't it be worth the effort to remember that once in a while?

The Flip Side

Perhaps the greatest burden Christianity adds to the burden of being a good human being and a grateful child of God is that, as we are forgiven, we ourselves must forgive. It's a burden we incautiously reaccept each time we say the Lord's Prayer. A moment that captures that difficult challenge is in the story of the prodigal son. The father forgives *before* the boy has a chance to get out his memorized confession. Remember from chapter 4:

No matter what our age, each of us still needs some matrix of meaning to hang on to, a background perspective against which everything can be measured so that it "makes sense." At least in the few moments we consecrate to getting our bearings, we need to feel, "It's okay, honey. Everything's just fine now."

We have a profound need for that. And, excepting sociopaths, so does everybody else.

Again, justice (morality) requires that, once atonement has been made, the debt disappears. Christianity (love) requires that, even though one demands restitution of the thief, the thief himself is forgiven before that. Even on a this-world, strictly human level, "resentment is like taking poison and hoping the other guy dies." But we also have to remember that the one whose myth we claim to revere as our own said, moments before he surrendered his Spirit to us: "Father, forgive them. They do not know what they are doing" (Luke 23:34).

EPILOGUE

Resurrecting Wonder

Rich: I'm not depressed! . . . I'm lamenting. I've lost my innocence.

Cromwell: You lost that some time ago. If you've only just noticed, it can't have been very important to you.
—*A Man for All Seasons*

An old psychology textbook had a wonderful frontispiece. The upper half pictured a cluster of babies: pink, sweet, delightful, innocent, exploring others' differences with their tiny fingertips. Below it was a picture of passengers in a subway car: taut, gray, sullen, sour, staring into the crowded emptiness. The caption asked simply, "What got lost?"

There you have this book, in three words.

What got lost was a soul, a self. Just as you got to the age and sensitivity and first-grasp of the skills to start getting to know it and putting it to use against "the slings and arrows of outrageous fortune," your soul most likely got smothered in more pressing concerns. (Enspiriting still might happen in college, but less probable, since for so many it's subsidized freedom while you learn the subtle skills of drinking beer, concussing your eardrums, and getting laid.) And truth-to-tell, most of the most intriguing, invigorating stuff has been discovered since we ourselves gave up thunder thinking. Life's to-be-gotten-through. As the great Indian Chief Seattle said in 1852, when the white men wanted to fill his opulent wilderness with the talking wires: "the end of living and the beginning of survival."

In a simpler world, no matter what anyone said, the *operative* incentives to the "eternal life" promised by Jesus were, in all frankness, fear of hell and hope of heaven. "Id motives." Not useless, but constrained to a level baser animals would also respond to. Perhaps some made a small step beyond total selfishness governed by loyalty to the family or the cohesion of the parish. But few of our mentors considered an internalized sense of justice or a need for personal integrity (beyond, and sometimes despite, the rules) to be likely motives for probity and loyalty to the common Christian enterprise. The soul was a precious burden, like an impaired child we had to protect from the ravages of hell, and even from the slightest smutch of evil along way. But after the Pentecostal inrush of fresh air from Vatican II, once the harsh focus of crime and punishment was arced down and finally dimmed, what motive was there left for formal religion? Or a soul?

"What got lost?" Our psyches, our souls, the life-giving essence of our humanity, the Atman-lodestar within us that led us on the Quest for the fulfillment we were separated from other animals in order to pursue. Authentic Christianity hardly had a snowball's chance.

Cave people's lives were simpler, cruder, unbearably harsher, but they were likely also more meaningful, more purposeful, more precious.

The little girl, waking in the dark, was bewildered, afraid. Native Americans, hauled by the hair into "civilization," were disoriented, perplexed, suddenly purposeless. Aldous Huxley anticipated it in *Brave New World.* Orwell foresaw it long before *1984,* which happened a generation ago. Alvin Tofler wrote *Future Shock* in 1970, showing that the acceleration of technological and social change had even then become so constant, so precipitous, so unstoppable that our limited souls and minds were unable to accommodate it. We were beginning to become disconnected and suffering from "shattering stress and disorientation." It's now forty years later. Our electron-accelerator brains are spinning so wildly they threaten to explode.

These pages maintained that the confirmation once vaunted to make us "adult Christians" failed to do so because we were incapable of either adulthood or Christianity. What's more, it prepared us for a feudal Catholic world that was beginning to fade out of existence even as we were fiddling with our pens and watching the clock. We hadn't been hurt enough yet to value freedom from fear of sin and death. We had unquestioningly digested a slicked-up, Potemkin-village version of "the Faith," plus the conviction that the yellow-brick road stretched on toward Oz with no red lights, and that we could succeed playing Monopoly (the only game in town) with honor bright and no shady deals. How laughably callow that sounds now.

We were too innocent to have even the faintest idea what Christianity really demanded or where the Culture of Materialism was really leading us. With a wondrous irony, back then we were too naive to see the bare truth. Now we're too sophisticated!

What Now, Then?

In 1940, W. H. Auden wrote a poem for the monument dedicated by the State to the ideal citizen of the future, which is now our present:

> [He] had everything necessary to the Modern Man,
> A phonograph, a radio, a car and a frigidaire....
> Was he free? Was he happy? The question is absurd:
> Had anything been wrong, we should certainly have heard.

The very first step toward liberating the dormant soul — the *sine qua non* — is admitting in our innermost, honest selves that "a phonograph, a radio, a car, and a frigidaire" are simply *not* enough. In the first place, they don't even have "phonographs" anymore, stupid. And old Auden didn't even know about TV, computers, iPads, cellphones, and Cialis. When he wrote that stupid poem, only freaks even knew about atomic bombs. And space flights were for kids' comics.

But Elvis Presley (for only one) had enough excess cash so that he could give a Cadillac convertible to a waitress for a tip. But he (among many others) defended himself from life, liberty, and the pursuit of happiness with drugs. Then he killed himself. Hooray.

Peggy Lee and Sisyphus both made the absolutely most fundamental claim any human being can come down to: there's gotta be *more* than just stuff and booze and havin' a ball! There's gotta be something that doesn't get stale, or snotty, or leave me in the lurch, something constant, substantial, coherent, lasting. Otherwise, "Stop the world! I want to get off!"

Face down all the temptations to paranoia, struggle at least to *want* a larger perspective than just "more." Convince yourself there must be a reality beyond Plato's cave and Helen Keller's secure darkness, and resolve to set out in Quest of it. Even if it costs. If you can bring yourself to the very unfashionable admission that "I'm missing something crucially important in the one life I have that I simply cannot purchase with money!" — then you can start.

That first step is negative. All the rest is positive!

Then the second step: Accepting "I am a soul, a self, a spark of the divine." That humans-only soul is real, but it's only *potential*. It won't activate, come alive, begin igniting a more than contented-animal life without my active, consistent effort.

Then the third step: resolving that actualizing that soul, that self, is worth conscious effort.

Seniors I've taught for the last forty-eight years sneer when I say there will come a time in their marriages when they have to make a deliberate resolution to have sex. They howl! *"Never!"* No one seems to have warned them about the life we are (supposedly) preparing them for — with spouses having different priorities and friends, bosses with unpleasant requests like promptness, clarity, the skills to outline, inconvenient and pressing deadlines, answers to questions no education offered pat answers for, kids' inconceivable values and priorities, mortgages, crabgrass, PMS, erectile dysfunction, sheer fatigue.

Then it should follow inexorably that any serious Catholic would have to be shaken up to be moved to find time to ponder. But it needn't wait for a tragedy, like losing a job, a spouse, a child. Wouldn't anyone claiming to be an intelligent, active participant in human life consider it essential to pull out of the rat race at least once a week and ask, "*Why* am I *doing* this — other than because I *have* to?" In the course of my dedication have I developed suppositions that aren't really as clear-eyed and well-reasoned as I'd thought? Where have I developed myopias? Against newcomers, people who are "different," nonconformist, smarter, nimbler-tongued? Is it just remotely possible that there's some tiniest kernel of truth in what the people I despise claim? Is what I've unquestioningly called "my faith" really just a matter of dull habit? Am I actually living merely a life of "propriety"?

Can I feel Gandalf the Grey or Glinda the Good stopping by my hut with an invitation to a life more exhilarating than self-protectiveness? Can I sense Jesus stopping by my upturned skiff and saying, "Let's push off!" Is there any honest sense that I'm not too old for a Quest?

Down-to-Earth Enchantments

> The woods are lovely, dark and deep.
> But I have promises to keep,
> And miles to go before I sleep,
> And miles to go before I sleep.
> — Robert Frost

This doesn't have to be, strictly speaking, prayer. At least not yet. But if you're not used to this kind of thing, it would probably be helpful to do it with pen and paper, even if you don't keep the result — because it gives you something concrete to come back to when you're distracted.

And, right here, we leave the theoretical for the down-to-earth. Or, more clumsily, practical ways to bring ungraspable truth into our everyday hands, in order to ignite our pedestrian weeks. (Or mixed metaphors along that line.) The rest is cookbook, how-to stuff, if you feel the need of it. If any part of what follows "clicks" — sends you off with an unexpected and faintly daunting need to explore — then you don't need me or any other book. In the going, you'll already be "there."

Your Treasury

Think of the one person who's the most precious person in your life. The person you'd be helpless not to forgive. The person who has enriched your existence more than anyone else has. Think of the shared secrets and shames. The accretions of trust that justified risking more together. What were the chances you might never have met? That you'd passed one another by as you have so many hundreds of thousands of others, day in, day out, without even fixating the face? How incredibly lucky! Rest there; embrace the presence, feel the energizing tingle of awareness of your good fortune. Force away any urge that asks, "What's next?" Just linger there, *feeling* blessed. Nothing wrong in that. It's what you were born for. Only when that warmth begins to dwindle, ask: "And who else has enriched me?" Move to the next face and dwell there in the memories. Stay. Quietly exult. Then ease on to the next. And the next. If you do that, I promise you'll be unable to feel sorry for yourself for a long, long time.

Wow!

Thanks!

The First Journey

Before you ever were, before your "isn't" became your "is," the two components of you were completely unacquainted. A single ovum sat like a grand duchess in her boudoir, packed with twenty-three unique chromosomes, and, unbeknownst to her about 500 million sperm (roughly the population of Europe) were speeding toward her at twenty-eight mph, each with his own cargo of twenty-three unique chromosomes and a single compelling purpose. And in that incredibly crowded marathon, only *one* succeeded (often, none did). What a wonderful bit of luck! Instantly, there was a new creation! An infinitesimally small new microcosmos. Then for a few days the fertilized ovum got passed gently along by tiny finger-like villi, like somebody passed overhead at a silent concert. Then you came to that precipitous edge above an enormous cave, where it was a 50–50 chance you'd snag onto the wall and embed yourself, doubling yourself there every day. Gasp! In eleven weeks, you were sucking your favorite thumb. By then, the miracles were coming too quickly to count, like discovering how to move and dream. For the remainder of the pregnancy, all kinds of DNA signals were snapping green: arm and leg buds, eyes, sex organs, the beginnings of a brain — and the whole miraculous you began to unfold, gratuitously, with no cooperation or certainly no merit on your part.

Wow!

Thanks!

Your Treasure-House

(You could do these as you work out, if you do.) Think of the miraculous body that enmeshes you, that's carried you from hither to yon, spears you through cool waters, bathes you in sweat on hot days, renews itself cell-by-cell every instant, sends emergency squads to every part when it's being attacked or weakened, urges you to passion, allows you to grin and weep and blush. Could you possibly comprehend all its multi-form, multi-functional, cooperating parts? (This one could take months.)

Plunge yourself in miracles and ponder your eyes. Two spherical jellies in the front of your face — two, so you can perceive in three dimensions! A transparent lens corrects for color and spherical distortion; a uniquely colored iris diaphragm fine-tunes focus continuously, even for impaired children. The retina's 125 million color-coding cells automatically switch among wavelengths. They take three-dimensional, color pictures as long as you can stay awake and never need developing or new film. Then those images converge into a brain that turns them into abstract ideas. And often if they're damaged they repair themselves.

Wow!

Thanks!

Then wander around that fascinating brain. Google it, if your introduction to its wonders was as skimpy as mine. There are 100,000 miles of blood vessels in that three-pound magic package, a hundred billion neurons, *each* with about five thousand connector-switches (synapses). New connections come into existence every time you reach for a new thought. So the more you think, the better you're able to think more. It needs less energy than your fridge light, but it uses 20 percent of your total oxygen intake. Even if you think your best thinking happens when you're grinding away with the old rational left brain, you probably get your richest ideas when you're just starting to come-to in the morning. They're called alpha waves. If somebody calls you "fathead," back off; 60 percent of your brain *is* fat. Computers are faster, but don't ask one whether it's legitimate to launch a hydrogen bomb. And your brain would keep on working even if every other electric source in the world went dead.

Wow!

Thanks!

Your Adventure Film

(Note: This ought not to be directed by some wimpy kid full of grandiose pretensions, fresh out of Columbia. You want somebody with depth and scope like Peter Jackson with the *Rings* or David Lean with *Lawrence of Arabia*.) First, picture yourself as Cinderella in her steamy scullery (or Hansel in his dark, dark cage). Linger a while in a tight shot and absorb the sense of degradation and futility. Then slowly pan back to the whole house with the stepsisters awaiting the "girl" to give them pedicures because (wide shot) the prince's carriage is hurtling around town with a crystal slipper. (Or pull back to Hansel's cave, and the gingerbread house now forthrightly sheathed in slime.) Pan back to a helicopter landscape shot swooping over all of Storyland. Our heroine (and hero) have shrunk to invisibility, though they still are, for the moment, "in our thoughts and concerns." Now really pull the POV dramatically out to a view backing off toward Jupiter, where the whole earth is just an amethyst globe crusted in clouds. But don't stop there! Keep going, out into a context no scriptural storyteller could have dreamed, even beyond the heretical imaginations of Copernicus and Galileo. By the time we can get the rings of Saturn into the shot, earth itself is pretty indistinguishable from all the other space grit. Oh, keep going. And going! What an excruciatingly gorgeous lightscape! Does anybody remember where this journey started? What was it "about"?

Ah, but there's more! The producers (at untold expense) have found a way to poke through *beyond* space and time! Once there, even the riotous fiery carouse of the universe is like a firefly to the smoldering sun. And at its center (though there's no such thing) is an Incandescent Presence with a voice as fierce as lava and gentle as dandelion fluff. And the voice says, "You got so deflected by all those fascinating distractions, you forgot what I did it all *for*. Go

back to Hansel and Cinderella. They're what's important to Me."
Surely, He/She/They are not *serious!*

Wow!

Thanks!

The Variety Show

This might happen if you dare waste time taking a walk in the
woods — maybe with a camera, because that somehow makes you
more observant. It also pacifies the still-unredeemed part of you
that *must* have a product to validate your existence. What you're
looking for is fascinating oddities: a two-colored flower or one
with two different sorts of petals, yucky worms, the silken trail
that betrays a snail's having passed. The kinds of things that *real*
kids exult in. (You might even rent-a-kid you can follow and learn
again how it's really done. As long as you reserve time later to
ponder and wonder about it on a level kids can't attain yet.)

Hopkins's poem catches it:

> Glory be to God for dappled things,
> For skies of couple-color as a brinded cow,
> For rose-moles all in stipple upon trout that swim;
> Fresh-firecoal chestnut-falls, finches' wings;
> Landscape plotted and pieced, fold, fallow and plough,
> And all trades, their gear and tackle and trim.
>
> All things counter, original, spare, strange,
> Whatever is fickle, freckled (who knows how?)
> With swift, slow; sweet, sour; adazzle, dim.
> He fathers-forth whose beauty is past change:
> Praise him.
> — Gerard Manley Hopkins

Did you ever realize there are no really *perfect* shapes in nature?
Not on this planet, or even — as far as we know yet — in the whole

universe. Not a single straight-line river, no perfect-triangle carrot or icicle, no circular lake. Crystals are wondrously free-form, and there's never been identical snowflakes — in all of Antarctica. Planetary orbits aren't circular but elliptical. Even the earth is a not-quite sphere. Thank God that God isn't a Cartesian rationalist (the kind who'll eventually itch to fine-tune the Beatific Vision). How grateful we should be that the Creator is so fanciful and inefficient! Wouldn't it be deadening if every apple were a perfect sphere, every tree as perfectly cylindrical as a flagpole, and every forester were Brad Pitt?

Wow!

Thanks!

Your Sacred Context

Home is a "sacred" place, even for the nonreligious. Just as religious people believe that, at the church doorsill, they step from secular into sacred space, all of us believe there's a special space beyond our own doorsills that simply cannot be violated. This is my place, where I can close the door on chaos and find some kind of cosmos, peace, belonging. "Home is," as Frost said, "the place where, when you go there, they have to take you in." Objects in that home are also "holy": a box of letters, an old photograph album, objects and pictures on your desk that say, "This is mine; here is a place I *belong.*"

Christmas is a "sacred" time even for those who do not practice or believe in religion. It's "a time to go home," to recapture a meaningful past where family made everything more or less "make sense." Thanksgiving and Christmas are the busiest times of the year for airlines: "Gotta get home! It's Christmas!" And without family, Christmas can be the most soul-harrowing time of the year. Christmas is also the busiest time for suicides — who die of "homesickness." We remember. And we want to go back when things were "right."

Slowly, as leisurely as you considered the people who enrich your being-alive, ponder one-by-one the places and times you hold "sacred, holy, inviolable." We're surrounded and penetrated and warmed by holiness like Helen Keller, all unaware in the sunshine.

Wow!

Thanks!

Your Confirmation Presents

Without doubt, you've forgotten the presents you received at confirmation from your baptismal sponsors (if they were even invited — or remembered) and from your maiden aunts (rosaries, ties, ribbons, books). According to Catholic folks who love lists, you received from the Holy Spirit the gifts of wisdom, understanding, counsel (prudence), courage, knowledge, piety (grateful service), and fear of the Lord (which I'd rather see translated as "awe"). I'd wager you once could rattle those off by memory. I could. But can you recall *feeling* them, either at the time or even today? Ponder each of them, separately, slowly — as you tried before to assimilate the meaning of all your dear ones. How are the reasons you couldn't appreciate them back then no longer legitimately operative now?

The fruits of the Holy Spirit — the tell-tale attitudes and habits that evidence her continuing effect in your life — are "love, joy, peace, patience, kindness, generosity, faithfulness, gentleness, and self-control" (Gal. 5:22–23). Just suppose such qualities were societally reprehensible, a cause of arrest and jury trial. Weigh each virtue, separately, and ask what concrete, specific, hard evidence "they" could get against you. I have a suspicion that, if you've read this far, the evidence is considerable.

Wow!

Thanks!

Your Glindas and Gandalfs

Someone taught you to read. Is she still alive, able to receive a thank-you card? Someone once said, at a critical moment, "That was well done." Someone (maybe more than once) rescued a computer file from oblivion for you. Someone may have refused to let you succumb to necrotizing fasciitis. Someone maybe cosigned a note with you. Someone said, "Thank you." Or "You'll never be alone." Or "You're forgiven."

Wow!

Thanks!

Your Passion

Martin Luther King Jr. wrote: "If a man has not found something worth dying for, he is not fit to live." Surely there are loved ones whose place you'd take in front of a firing squad. You might be willing to die for your country, even when the cause was not only futile but wrong. But is there any idea, any principle, for which you'd yield your life rather than publicly deny? With absolute honesty, I would not elect death rather than foreswear papal infallibility or the Immaculate Conception or the Assumption. But I'd die (at least I hope I would) rather than deny the divinity of Jesus and his (somehow) complete presence in the Eucharist — since they have been the bulwarks of my nearly eighty years, my validation, and my incentive to keep going.

"Passion" is a prickly reality. On the one hand, for old-timers, it has a strong aroma of forbidden lust. On the other, for the newly sophisticated, it's a trifle, well, unnerving — like anyone overly enthusiastic about, well, anything. Unless you make peace with the fiery Id, the inescapable animal inside, it won't go away. Instead, it will retreat deep inside and gain heat and bluster, and will inevitably burst out in grumpiness, testiness, bitchiness. But, far more important, is it in any way possible (at least honorably) to dismiss passion in a belief-system whose Founder's entire climactic week was called his "Passion"?

Wow?

Thanks?

Finally (Well, Not Really)

Once upon a time there was a Jesuit named Ed Cuffe. His soul was so lightsome he probably should have been fitted for iron shoes to keep him from drifting off like some errant multicolored balloon. He taught English. At least that's what he lapsed into when he wasn't skipping stones on ponds or standing transfixed by a butterfly.

A seminarian named Jim Kelly knew he himself was a very bright young fellow but just couldn't get an acceptably exhilarating grade from Ed. So he asked if he could do extra reading.

"Oh, uh, sure. Go to the library."

Huh? "What book shall I get?"

"Oh, uh, I dunno. Poke around and find something interesting."

"Well, what should I do then?"

"Read it."

Jim giggled with embarrassment. "And what will that add to my grade?"

And Ed answered quietly, "Delight?"

It's right there. But you have to reach for it.